P9-BTY-369

Electric Cars

Electric Cars

BY E. JOHN DE WAARD
AND AARON E. KLEIN

8407
629.2
D

Blairsville Junior High School
Blairsville, Pennsylvania

Doubleday & Company, Inc.
Garden City, New York

ACKNOWLEDGMENTS

The authors gratefully acknowlege the assistance of Harrah's Auto Collection, Reno, Nevada; the Wisner Family Archives, Manchester, Michigan; and Mr. Nicholas Rosa in the preparation of the manuscript.

This book is part of a Museum of Science & Industry/Chicago series of science books published by Doubleday & Company, Incorporated. The series is designed to inform, stimulate, and challenge youngsters on a wide range of scientific and technological subjects.

Library of Congress Cataloging in Publication Data

De Waard, E. John.
  Electric cars.

  (Chicago's Museum of Science and Industry/Doubleday series)
  Includes index.
  SUMMARY: Introduces the history and operation of electric cars, vehicles in limited use for many years that are attracting renewed attention as one possible solution to the energy crisis.
  1. Automobiles, Electric—Juvenile literature.
[1. Automobiles, Electric]   I. Klein, Aaron E., joint author.   II. Title.   III. Series.
TL220.D43   629.22'93
Library of Congress Catalog Card Number 74-18790
ISBN 0-385-00962-3 Trade
      0-385-08143-X Prebound

Copyright © 1977 by E. John De Waard and Aaron E. Klein
All Rights Reserved
Printed in the United States of America
9 8 7 6 5 4 3

Contents

Electric Cars

1

THE RISE AND FALL
OF THE ELECTRIC CAR

Imagine that you are a driver caught up in an oil shortage. You
have been waiting in a line at a gas station for over an hour,
hoping that the price of the gas won't go up again before you
get to the pumps. In the rear-view mirror you see a small vehicle of unfamiliar make. Right away you can see that the driver
has no intention of getting into the gas line. The little car stops

for a traffic light. Strange indeed is the automobile. There are no exhaust fumes. In fact, there is no exhaust pipe.

If there is no exhaust pipe, you think, the driver must have lost his muffler. But if he had lost his muffler that car would be making an awful racket, yet there is a strange lack of noise. The car starts up as the light changes, but you still do not hear the clatter of an unmuffled engine. You think you can detect a low hum.

It is then that you realize that the vehicle is an electric car. Now that you think about it, you remember your grandfather talking about the electric car *his* father drove back in the early 1900s. Why aren't there any electric cars around now?

But there *are* electric cars around today. Most of them, however, are disguised. A golf cart is an electric vehicle. Thousands of electric forklift vehicles are used in factories all over the world. And there are a few electric passenger cars and delivery vans running around on the streets and highways.

The distinction between "vehicle" and "car" is an important one. Locomotives and trolley cars are self-propelled vehicles, but they cannot go everywhere; they can go only where the tracks are. "Car" can mean the same thing as "automobile" and, in this book, it almost always will, if for no other reason than to get away from using the word automobile all the time. However, a "car" can be a railroad car, an elevator car, an aerial-lift car (the sky ride of amusement parks), or the part of a blimp you ride in.

Ever since human beings have had enough brain to think, they have wanted to figure out ways of getting places and getting things done without using their own muscles. For hundreds of thousands of years, people walked or ran if they wanted to travel. At least ten thousand years ago, possibly earlier, some people were using the muscles of horses and other animals to move about and do work. No one knows when and where wheels were first made and used, but somewhere, at some time, hooking up animals to wheeled vehicles added a new dimension to travel and to moving goods from one place to another on land.

For thousands of years, through most of recorded history, animals were the chief means of transportation on land. But dreams of some kind of vehicle that would go by itself, with no horse pulling it or wind blowing it, are as old as or older than history. The ancient folk tales of many people are filled with legends of flying carpets, seven-league boots, and soaring chariots. The dream has been a reality for hardly two hundred years.

For hundreds of years, men toyed and tinkered with numerous mechanical devices in hopes of inventing a machine which would take the place of animals. In the fifteenth century, the great Leonardo da Vinci considered the possibilities of such a machine. He was probably the first man ever to design an armored vehicle. This was intended for use as a military weapon. Its four wheels were rotated from the inside by men turning cranks. Sketches of this vehicle look curiously like the flying saucer of science fiction. Of course, Da Vinci's car could hardly be called a self-propelled vehicle. But it is noteworthy that Leonardo conceived of the idea of the motive force *inside* the vehicle rather than pulling from outside.

In the 1600s, an inventor in Holland named Simon Steven designed a sailing chariot. Actually, it looked less like a chariot than like a boat with four wheels. Two broad sails hoisted to catch the wind were supposed to furnish the power for this vehicle. The greatest problem, of course, was the wind. Such a craft could move in only one direction and only when the wind blew.

Another experimental vehicle of the 1600s was the Nuremberg car. This ornately gilded carriage was operated by a clock spring. The greatest handicap in traveling with this car was that every few minutes the passenger had to get out and rewind the spring. The passenger would have been better off with a horse, since he was actually putting his own energy into moving the vehicle.

The main problem in all of these early vehicles was that of finding a reliable source of power. Steam engines were the first power plants to be used successfully in self-propelled vehicles. Sir Isaac Newton suggested the possibility of steam propulsion as early as 1670, but more than a hundred years would go by before steam-powered vehicles became a reality. To show how it might be done, he had constructed a small steam boiler and a steam jet. Two years earlier, in 1678, the great Dutch physicist Christiaan Huygens had described the first internal-combustion engine. It consisted of a cylinder and a piston powered by burning gunpowder.

The first truly self-propelled vehicle was a monstrous-looking steam carriage built by Nicholas Cugnot in 1769. Cugnot was a French artillery officer whose experiments with steam propulsion had come to the attention of the French minister of war. He was authorized by the minister to design a machine which would drag cannon onto the battlefield. Cugnot's carriage was almost useless for that or any other purpose. Its top speed was three miles an hour, and it usually boiled dry within ten minutes. But it proved one thing: a self-propelled vehicle was a possibility.

Other inventors were quick to see the possibilities of the steam-powered vehicle. Oliver Evans of Philadelphia received the first American patent for a self-propelled steam vehicle in 1789. Richard Trevithick built England's first full-sized steam carriage in 1801. For a brief period there were steam-carriage lines that threatened to force horse-drawn stagecoaches out of business. But steam carriages proved to be too heavy and expensive to run for profitable operation as road vehicles. Heavy steam engines needed to be supported by rails. They sank in the mud of the unpaved roads of the time. Railroads proved to be greatly profitable, and steam engines were soon earning their keep on rail lines all over the world. Interest in making self-propelled road vehicles died down in the nineteenth century. It was not until the 1880s and thereafter that there were again serious efforts at making what we would today call an automobile.

The earliest automobiles were powered by internal-combustion engines. Steam engines are combustion engines too. Combustion is just a fancy word for burning. Steam engines, however, are *external*-combustion engines. That is, the burning takes place outside the engine. A fuel such as coal is burned to heat water in a boiler. The resulting steam is piped to cylinders where it pushes pistons to provide the motive power. As you might expect, internal-combustion engines are those in which the fuel is burned right inside the cylinder. The hot, expanding gases that result from the burning push a piston which supplies the motive power.

The idea of internal-combustion engines was not new in the 1870s and 1880s. Such engines had been proposed even before Newton suggested steam engines. The advantages of internal combustion over external combustion were obvious even in the 1670s. Since internal-combustion engines did not need heavy boilers, they could be lighter and therefore more suitable for road use. They also had the promise of more economical operation than steam engines.

However, internal combustion presented many engineering problems which were beyond the capabilities of eighteenth-century and early-nineteenth-century technology. First of all, if something is to be burned inside a cylinder, the fuel had better burn completely or nearly completely. Otherwise, the cylinder will soon become fouled with ashes. Also needed were materials that could withstand the tremendous heat generated by internal combustion. There were neither fuels nor metals that could meet these criteria in the eighteenth century.

Nevertheless, there were attempts to make internal-combustion engines in the early 1800s. In 1807, Isaac de Rivaz in France assembled an engine that featured a piston moved by an exploding mixture of hydrogen and air.

The steam engines that flourished in the Industrial Revolution of the eighteenth and nineteenth centuries ran on coal and wood. Internal-combustion engines could not begin to compete seriously with steam engines until the discovery of petroleum and the further discovery that fuels such as gasoline could be distilled out of the petroleum. And all of this did not happen until after the middle of the nineteenth century.

Serious renewed interest in internal-combustion engines began around 1860. A number of fuels, such as naphtha, alcohol, hydrogen, and even gunpowder were tried. But gasoline proved to be the most effective and economical fuel. In 1875 an Austrian named Siegfried Marcus built a small vehicle powered by an internal-combustion engine. It worked, but there is no evidence that anyone bought one. In the 1880s, Karl Benz in Germany was making internal-combustion engines and attaching them to tricycle-like vehicles. He sold some of his machines. Gottlieb Daimler, another German, was also active in the internal-combustion field at about the same time.

At first people thought that these noisy, sputtering, and dangerous "horseless carriages" were merely curiosities that would never be competition for horses and railroad trains. But the idea caught on. There were enough people intrigued with the idea of a self-propelled vehicle that could go anywhere, any time. Most importantly, there were enough people willing to spend the money to buy these vehicles, unreliable and dangerous as they were. By the turn of the century there was no longer any doubt that the horseless carriage, or automobile, was here to stay for a long time.

As soon as it became obvious that automobiles were not a passing fancy and were, therefore, potentially profitable, literally thousands of people went into the automobile business. These enterprises ranged from tinkerers in barns to huge corporations. Early automobiles were moved by a variety of power sources. Steam technology was certainly widely available at the turn of the century and had benefited from almost two hundred years of development. There were soon many steam-powered cars on the road, and in the early days most steam cars were far more dependable than those powered by gasoline engines. There was something else around in the early 1900s that could make things move, and that was the electric motor.

Electricity was in wide use by 1900, especially in cities. Thomas Edison had invented his electric light bulb in 1876. By the 1880s, electricity was supplied to thousands of customers from central power stations. Electric motors were used also in factories to run machinery, and starting around the 1880s there were hundreds of electric vehicles operating in cities and between cities. These were trolley cars. Electric-motor technology was far more advanced than gasoline-engine technology around 1900.

Experimentation with electricity had started in earnest soon after steam engines started the Industrial Revolution in the early 1800s. At the outset, interest in electricity was purely a matter of scientific curiosity. Benjamin Franklin's interest in electricity is well known. In 1800 an Italian scientist, Alessandro Volta, had made and experimented with what is now called the voltaic pile. The voltaic pile was a stack of metal disks and salt-water soaked rags which produced an electric current. It was the precursor of the modern electrical cell or battery. In 1820 Hans Oersted, a Danish physics teacher, accidentally discovered that magnetic fields are associated with electric currents.

By the middle of the nineteenth century there were two main ways known to produce enough electricity to do useful work. One was the chemical cell, which produced electricity by chemical action. The other was electromagnetic induction. In the latter, electricity is made by spinning a coil of wire in a magnetic field. The machine that produces electricity by induction is called a generator or dynamo. The electric motor was soon to follow after the discovery of electromagnetic induction.

In fact, electric motors were available long before they were economical to use. Joseph Henry, an American, made an electric motor in 1836.

So by the time there were enough buyers around to make automobile manfacturing profitable, three major ways of making automobiles go were available—internal combustion, steam, and electricity. And in the 1890s and 1900s the most efficient street vehicles of all were electric streetcars. The earliest electric street-railway cars were powered by storage batteries. But it was soon seen that supplying power from overhead wires or wires in the track was much more dependable than batteries. The power was picked up from the overhead wires by a grooved wheel called a "troller," from which the word trolley evolved.

The existence of the electric trolley car contributed a great deal to the acceptance of electric cars. At least people knew an electric motor would work and that it was much less likely to blow up than a steam engine or a gasoline engine. In 1900 an electric motor was a much more dependable mechanism than were most gasoline engines.

By the 1900s there was an extensive network of electric trolley-car lines. In fact, a traveler had many choices of dependable transportation, and automobiles—electric, steam, or gasoline —were the least dependable. For travel between cities, there were railroads. In most cities, large, medium, and small, it was possible to get on a trolley car right at the railroad station and go almost anywhere in the city. Many trolley lines ran between cities in competition with railroads. So it would seem that automobiles were not the necessities they are today.

Yet, in spite of their expense and lack of reliability, automobiles achieved great popularity in a relatively short period of

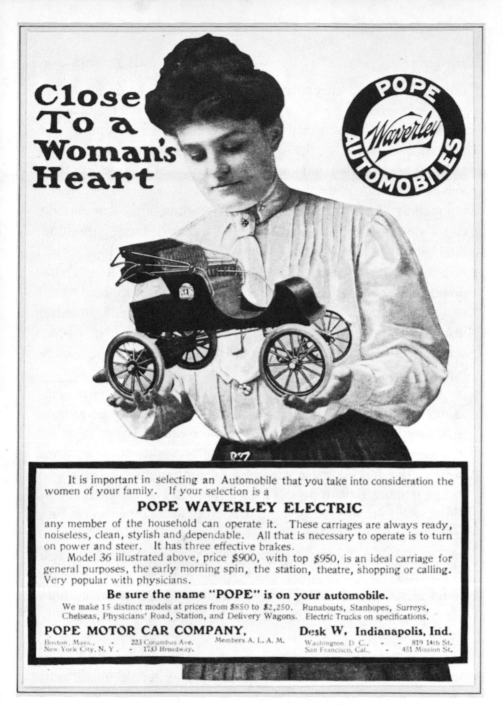

Close To a Woman's Heart

POPE *Waverley* **AUTOMOBILES**

It is important in selecting an Automobile that you take into consideration the women of your family. If your selection is a

POPE WAVERLEY ELECTRIC

any member of the household can operate it. These carriages are always ready, noiseless, clean, stylish and dependable. All that is necessary to operate is to turn on power and steer. It has three effective brakes.

Model 36 illustrated above, price $900, with top $950, is an ideal carriage for general purposes, the early morning spin, the station, theatre, shopping or calling. Very popular with physicians.

Be sure the name "POPE" is on your automobile.

We make 15 distinct models at prices from $850 to $2,250. Runabouts, Stanhopes, Surreys, Chelseas, Physicians' Road, Station, and Delivery Wagons. Electric Trucks on specifications.

POPE MOTOR CAR COMPANY,   Members A. L. A. M.   **Desk W. Indianapolis, Ind.**

Boston, Mass.,   -   223 Columbus Ave.   Washington D C.,   -   -   819 14th St.
New York City, N. Y.   -   1733 Broadway.   San Francisco, Cal.,   -   451 Mission St.

The object of the lady's seeming adoration is a 1906 Pope Waverley Model 36. This attempt to market the electric car as a "woman's car" was typical of the period. This 1906 stanhope was about in the middle of the Pope-Waverley line. The history of the Pope Motor Company was also typical of the period. It was reorganized, merged, discontinued, re-established, and so on at least ten times from 1896 to 1914. Pioneer auto-making companies reorganized frequently in attempts to capture markets, or because partners split up in anger. The company made a wide variety of electric vehicles, including a limousine with a 7½-foot wheel base.

time. Why would anyone give up a dependable five-cent trolley ride for a wheezing, clanking collection of unperfected machinery that might cost around two thousand dollars or more? Two thousand dollars was a lot of money in 1900. You could buy a good house for that amount, and many people lived comfortably on less than two thousand dollars a year. Yet there was a compelling reason for wanting an automobile. Automobiles could do something trolley cars and railroad trains could not do. Automobiles could take you where you wanted to go when you wanted to go there. Never mind that they frequently broke down or got stuck in the mud holes that were supposed to be roads. The appeal was that they held the promise of providing instant mobility in privacy, with *you* in control. There was no waiting for trolley cars, no gearing your life to a railroad timetable.

Automobiles also held the promise of being particularly useful in rural areas that did not have trolley cars or railroad lines nearby. Farmers could get their produce to market much more quickly than they could with horse-drawn wagons. And farmers did indeed make great use of automobiles. They were used for more than transportation. Farmers hooked them up to plows. The engines were used to pump water, saw wood, and perform a variety of other farm chores.

You might think that automobiles would have been relatively scarce in cities. Such was not the case. City dwellers who could afford them, eagerly acquired automobiles. Soon automobiles joined the other vehicles competing for space on city streets.

If you could have visited a large city such as New York around 1912, you would have found a noisy tangle of all kinds of horse-drawn carriages and wagons, electric trolley cars, gasoline automobiles, steam automobiles, and electric automobiles. The heavy traffic usually kept them from moving very fast, but they made up for their slow pace with noise.

The Borland 1913 Regular Coupe—
A beautiful and elegant production $2900

Specifications: General Electric motor, especially built for us to withstand a 500% overload. General Electric non-arcing controller with 6 speeds forward and 3 reverse. Wheel base 96 inches. Extra large aluminum 5-passenger body, revolving front seats, either front or rear drive. *Batteries:* 40 cells, 9 plate Exide. *Speed:* 22 miles per hour. *Equipment:* Skid chains, hydrometer, odometer, toilet case and flower vase. Solid or pneumatic tires, optional, 34 x 4.

The new Borland models are now ready

THEY are equipped with the new Borland simplicity horizontal control, the greatest improvement for controlling speed.

The inconvenience in many electric automobiles has been the necessity of pulling up a lever or pressing a button or pushing a pedal to reverse. The Borland control [patent applied for] is the simplest and easiest to operate. No levers, no pedals, no buttons. And for appearance, satisfaction, comfort, safety, speed, convenience and *mileage*, the Borland is the most convincing electric known.

You can drive the Borland with absolute safety and freedom from worry—because of the simplest control of any electric, the clearest view of the road, the quickest action of our improved foot brakes and the positive assurance of an immediate response from every part of the machine.

The Borland 1913 Outside Drive Limousine—the Electric De Luxe $5500

Specifications: General Electric motor, especially designed and built for us to withstand a 500% overload. Specially designed, non-arcing controller with 6 speeds forward and 3 reverse. Wheel base, 121 inches. Seven-passenger body, exclusively designed and built for us by C. P. Kimball & Co. *Batteries:* 42 cells, 19 plate Exide. *Speed:* 25 miles per hour. *Equipment:* Skid chains, hydrometer, toilet case and flower vase, umbrella to match upholstery, odometer, 36 x 5 pneumatic tires with quick detachable rims. Klaxonet horn.

The Borland Electric Pre-Eminent Construction

Since the first Borland was made we have concentrated on the designing, building and perfecting of one chassis. We are finally satisfied that the Borland chassis represents the best engineering ideas and the correct selection of metals for each and every part. The proof of the efficiency of this chassis is our long list of satisfied customers.

Now that every engineering and service test has proved that every detail of Borland construction is right, we are putting out six new models, built on the same mechanical principles which made the Borland Brougham so satisfactory and successful.

Besides the two models illustrated we are making: Brougham, $2500, Coupe, $2700, either front or rear drive; Roadster, $2550; 1500-pound delivery truck, open body, $2100; 1500-pound truck, with closed body, $2250. These models make a complete line for dealers to handle. Write for poster booklet and catalog explaining the full meaning of the above improvements and the pre-eminence of Borland construction and design.

Exhibit at the Chicago Show, Space A-1, First Regiment Armory

The Borland-Grannis Co.

Salesrooms: 2642 Michigan Avenue   Chicago   Factory: East Huron Street

Dealers: Start the new year right. Do a twelve month business without increasing your overhead, selling Borland Electrics. We are closing with many established dealers. Write today for particulars. Or, better still, see U. B. Grannis, Vice President, at the Waldorf Hotel, during the New York Show. He will be pleased to give dealers full information concerning the Borland Line.

The Borland-Grannis Company made exceptionally high-quality, luxurious electric cars. The company was in business for only ten years, 1903–13. Borlands were among the few electric cars with shaft drive rather than chain drive. The motors were made by the General Electric Company to the specifications of the car manufacturer. Many electric-car makers used whatever existing motors they could get at the lowest prices.

The body of the 1913 "regular coupe" was made of aluminum. The two Borlands were equipped with simple "horizontal" controls. That is, forward or reverse direction change was accomplished with a single control. The coupe had six forward and three reverse speeds. It could be driven from the front or the back.

Columbia
Automobiles
Electric ❧ Gasoline

Write for new 24-page Catalogue illustrating and describing 17 different Columbia Automobiles for all requirements of pleasure or business. Special Booklet about Broughams.

Electric Vehicle Co.
Hartford, Conn.

NEW YORK - 100 Broadway
BOSTON - 43-45 Columbus Ave.
CHICAGO - 1421 Michigan Ave.

Columbia electrics were made from 1875 to 1916. The company also made gasoline cars. This is an early Columbia enclosed brougham. 1902.

Horses' hooves clattered and clopped on the stone pavement, but as noise-makers they were pitifully inferior to gasoline cars. Most gasoline cars of the time shattered the atmosphere with their racket. They banged, popped, sputtered, and boomed their way through the streets. Most had mufflers, but most of those with mufflers had "cut outs." That is, the exhaust gases could be vented directly out of the engine if the driver so chose. And far too many drivers so chose. It was widely believed that the engine operated more efficiently and economically without a muffler. Manufacturers advised, however, that the mufflers be used in the city and that unmuffled operation be limited to the countryside. Few drivers made the distinction. Electrically powered trolley cars added the clang of bells, the screech of steel wheel on steel track, and the rhythmic pounding of their air compressors. The latter supplied compressed air to operate the brakes. Steam cars sort of huffed and puffed like the miniature locomotives that they were.

In the chaos of a city street in 1912 electric cars seemed almost silent. But they were not completely silent. Some of them had a rather high-pitched whine from the transmission gears or chains that transmitted the power from the motor to the wheels. But the whine of an electric car was no match against gasoline cars, horses' hooves, and trolley cars.

The relative silence of electric cars provided much of their appeal. They were also much cleaner in operation than other kinds of cars. They achieved their greatest success in cities. Wealthy society ladies preferred them for short trips around the city, shopping and visiting and going to the theater.

Electric cars could not begin to match the speed of gasoline and steam cars. But that was fine for driving around the city. As we have seen, heavy traffic seldom allowed for high speeds in city streets. There were few if any expressways in the 1910s. Electric cars were also much easier to handle than gasoline and steam cars, another circumstance which contributed to their wide use by women. Most gasoline engines of the 1910s had to be cranked by hand to start. Hand cranking could be dangerous. Sometimes the crank handle "kicked back," breaking a wrist or an occasional jaw. Danger aside, hand cranking was not considered a ladylike thing to do. The cumbersome, massive clothing that was the style for women in the 1910s made hand cranking difficult for them.

Electric cars were started by flipping a switch. Steam cars did not require cranking, but they did require patience. You had to wait for the water to boil and to get up a good "head" of steam. And you had to think about what you were doing while you drove them.

Of all the cars available in the first twenty years of the century, electric cars were among the most luxurious. Many of them were literally parlors on wheels. Often there were no front and back seats; driver and passengers sat together on a curved couchlike seating arrangement or in separate lounge chairs in a compartment that looked somewhat like an oversized telephone booth on wheels. Some had chairs that swiveled. In many, the driver sat to the rear rather than the front. Really deluxe models had soft, overstuffed upholstery, velvet curtains, crystal flower vases, and other elegant appointments.

Manufacturers of electric vehicles did not limit themselves to luxurious passenger cars. There were also many makes of electric trucks. These ranged from small delivery vans to trucks which carried loads of five tons or more.

The makers of electric cars prospered in the early twentieth century along with the makers of gasoline and steam cars. Some companies made all types of cars—gasoline, steam, and electric. Yet by the 1930s electric cars were things of the past, relics of a faded age. Steam cars were also history. The gasoline engine was undisputed master of the streets and roads. What happened?

Basically what happened is that the electric car just could

Columbia ELECTRIC BROUGHAMS

Universally Recognized as the Ideal Closed Carriage for Private Service Irrespective of Make or Motive Power

Suitable for All Occasions
Reliable in All Weathers

THIS COLUMBIA ELECTRIC BROUGHAM, Mark 68, is a leading representative of the Columbia Line. The interior is lined throughout with heavy, dark-green broadcloth. The furnishings include silk curtains, dome electric light, card case, memorandum pad, mirror, toilet case, umbrella holder, driver's electric signal and speaking-tube connecting with driver's seat. The body is painted in rich and lustrous combinations of green and black. The electric side lamps and rear lamp are of the most approved pattern.

Catalogue on request, describing Columbia Broughams, Landaulets, Hansoms, Victorias, Victoria-Phaetons

ELECTRIC VEHICLE COMPANY, Hartford, Conn.

REPOSITORIES:

NEW YORK BRANCH: Electric Vehicle Co., 134-136-138 West 39th Street
CHICAGO BRANCH: Electric Vehicle Co., 1332-1334 Michigan Avenue
BOSTON: The Columbia Motor Vehicle Co., Trinity Place and Stanhope St.

Member A. L. A. M.

A 1907 Columbia enclosed brougham. Broughams were designed to be driven by a chauffeur exposed to the weather. Passengers and driver communicated via a speaking tube.

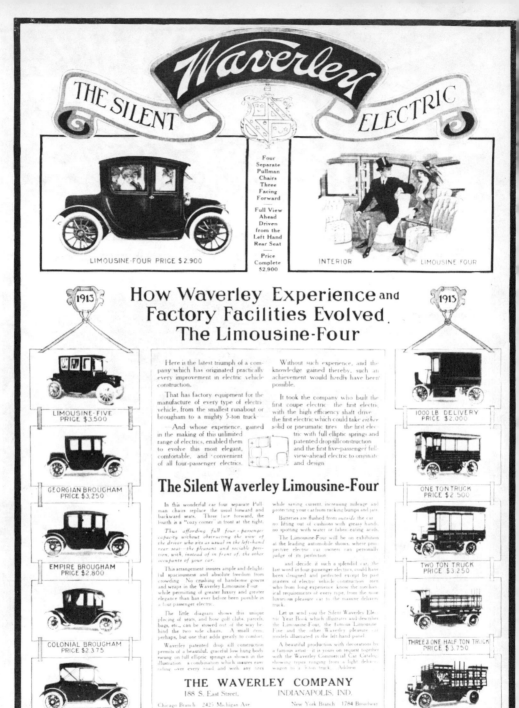

This 1913 ad shows the wide range of electric vehicles offered by one company. The Waverley Company was one of the reorganizations of the Pope Waverley Company. The interiors of the Limousine-Four, Limousine-Five, and broughams were quite luxurious. With lines in the ad such as "no crushing of handsome gowns and wraps," the company went after the luxury market. The company went out of business for the last time in 1914.

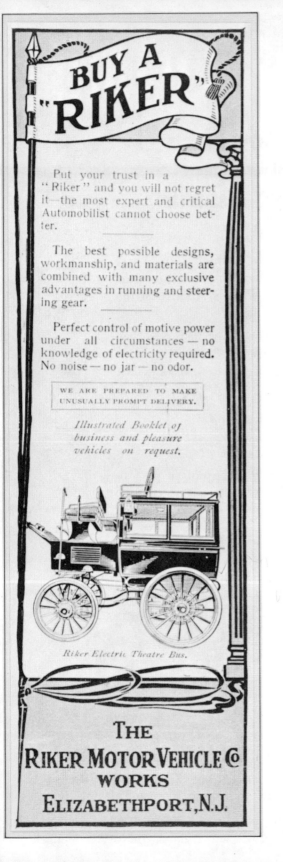

BUY A "RIKER"

Put your trust in a "Riker" and you will not regret it—the most expert and critical Automobilist cannot choose better.

The best possible designs, workmanship, and materials are combined with many exclusive advantages in running and steering gear.

Perfect control of motive power under all circumstances — no knowledge of electricity required. No noise — no jar — no odor.

WE ARE PREPARED TO MAKE UNUSUALLY PROMPT DELIVERY.

Illustrated Booklet of business and pleasure vehicles on request.

Riker Electric Theatre Bus.

THE RIKER MOTOR VEHICLE CO WORKS ELIZABETHPORT, N.J.

The 1900 Riker Theatre Bus. A. L. Riker sold electric cars for only a short time, 1896–1900. But in that short time he made significant contributions to electric-car technology. One of his first electric cars, a two-seater phaeton, won a race competing against several gasoline cars. Another of his electrics, a torpedo-shaped racer, set a new speed record for electrics in 1900—a mile in one minute and forty-six seconds. In addition to the bus, Riker made a two-seater runabout, a four-seater dos-à-dos (two passengers facing front and two facing to the rear), and heavy trucks. Riker merged with the Electric Vehicle Company, maker of Columbia electrics, in late 1900.

Rauch & Lang Electrics
on Exhibit at the
Waldorf-Astoria
"Turkish Room"

From January 6th to 15th, in New York, during the National Automobile Show, our cars will be shown at the Waldorf-Astoria, in the comfortable "Turkish Room."

Readers of this announcement who are in New York at that time are cordially urged to inspect them.

This unusual exhibit itself is interesting and it exhibits an unusual car.

The Rauch & Lang meets every requirement of most people's definition of the word "correct."

Call at the Waldorf-Astoria between January 6th and 15th, and see if it doesn't meet yours.

Rauch & Lang Electrics

THE RAUCH & LANG
CARRIAGE COMPANY
2351 West 25th St. **Cleveland** *Sixth City*

Additional exhibits at our New York Branch Showroom, Broadway and 58th Street.

Exide Battery standard equipment. Special Electric Pneumatic or Motz High-Efficiency Cushion Tires optional.

(118)

A 1912 Rauch and Lang brougham. Rauch and Lang lasted longer in the electric-car business than most others, starting in 1905 and making their last car in 1928. An old established carriage firm, the company was a leader in the horse-drawn-vehicle field. Among the largest of the Rauch and Lang electrics was a six-seater limousine. Rauch and Lang electrics were among the few that had four gears.

This car gives you a new set of reasons for owning an electric

A car of French design of the very latest fashion. Guaranteed for life. Design protected by letters patent.

$1750

You've always felt, in all probability, that you would like to own an electric car, if you could.

But the Hupp-Yeats confronts you with an entirely new set of reasons, which haven't existed before.

You've probably said—or your wife has—"If I can't have the best and the most beautiful, I don't want any—and $2500 or $3000 is more than we can afford."

The Hupp-Yeats overcomes that objection to begin with; because it brings you the service and the beauty that heretofore have required around $1000 additional.

That's New Reason No. 1.

New Reason No. 2 is a dignity of design due to the low-hung coach—which came into being with the Hupp-Yeats and is peculiar to it.

HUPP-YEATS
ELECTRIC

New Reason No. 3 is the elimination of some 400 pounds of weight—with all that that means in power-saving and the consequent cost of keeping the car.

New Reason No. 4 is the direct transmission of power from motor to axle—axle and motor being practically a single unit. This feature alone intensifies immensely the desirability of the electric, because it eliminates the loss of power due to the use of the ordinary chain drive.

New Reason No. 5 is the 50% reduction of wind resistance due to the sloping hood and curved roof—another element in the economy of current and cost of upkeep.

New Reason No. 6 is the entirely original factor of safety presented by the low-hung body—a feature which reduces the danger of skidding 75% and makes it impossible for the Hupp-Yeats to overturn.

So, when you come to decide now, whether you can or cannot afford an electric, the Hupp-Yeats makes claims upon your consideration which forbid you to judge it by any other car.

If you inquire into these unique Hupp-Yeats features, you'll say "Yes."

Therefore, let us send you the literature.

The Hupp-Yeats is driven by a Westinghouse motor. It is capable of a speed of 17 to 20 miles per hour and a mileage range of 75 to 90 miles per charge of the Exide Hycap batteries. The Westinghouse controller provides five speeds forward and two reverse. The tires are Goodyear long distance No-Rim-Cut.

R. C. H. SALES COMPANY, 117 Lycaste Street, DETROIT, MICHIGAN
BRANCHES IN THE FOLLOWING CITIES:
BUFFALO, 1125 Main Street; CHICAGO, 1509 Michigan Avenue; CLEVELAND, 2039 Euclid Avenue; DENVER, 1620 Broadway; DETROIT, Woodward and Warren Avenues; KANSAS CITY, 34th Street and Broadway; MINNEAPOLIS, 1334 Nicollet Avenue; PHILADELPHIA, 330 N. Broad St.; LOS ANGELES.

The 1911 Hupp-Yeats. Hupp-Yeats was a relative latecomer in the electric-car field. The company made electrics from 1911 to 1916. The main marketing thrust was low price. Electrics had an image as the stately, dignified, slow-moving vehicles of the rich and aristocratic. Hupp-Yeats offered the image at a price considerably less than the price of most closed-body electrics. For its low price, Hupp-Yeats did offer many desirable mechanical features, such as direct drive, not found in more expensive electrics. The company provided a "life guarantee."

Here Is a Car That Is The Culmination of Ripe Experience and Earnest Endeavor

ELEVEN years of earnest devotion to an ideal have culminated in the production of an electric car that stands alone—the Car Luxurious.

Wonderfully graceful of line, it is rich and beautiful of finish—marvelous in the simplicity of its operation—truly the most perfect electric car that engineering and mechanical genius have ever produced.

Eleven long years have been devoted to the development of this remarkable car—eleven years of experience are back of it—eleven years of steadfast determination to produce an electric car of unapproached beauty and efficiency are represented in it.

Ask the owners who bought the car five, eight, ten years ago.

They will tell you of the wonderful reliability and durability of the car—of the year-after-year service that

it has given them—of the honest workmanship that has given perfection to every detail of construction.

They will tell you of its easy-riding qualities, the beauty of its finish, the roominess of its interior, the reserve power and durability of its motor.

No Phipps-Grinnell owner has ever been willing to change to an electric of any other make. And now, for the first time, the result of these eleven years of successful endeavor is offered to the public in a general way. Heretofore, sales have been limited to fifteen or twenty cars a year. The 1911 production will not exceed 250 to 300 cars. We are not striving for a large output, quality always has been and always will be the dominant feature.

The Phipps-Grinnell Electric is exceptionally roomy, carrying five persons comfortably and giving ample space between the seats. The cushions are large and deep and roomy, upholstered in best-quality goat-skin—the springs are unusually long and especially tempered to give the maximum resiliency that makes the Phipps-Grinnell the easiest-riding car in America.

The Phipps-Grinnell is the *only* electric car with complete chain-in-oil drive, dust-proof and noiseless—almost frictionless, and eliminating entirely the excessive loss of power that is inevitable in shaft-driven vehicles.

The Phipps-Grinnell Electric is the *only* electric car with the foot-pedal reverse. It is never necessary to remove hands from controller or steering-handle for any forward or reverse speed.

In ease of operation, in simplicity of construction, in efficiency and reliability of its motive power, the Phipps-Grinnell stands alone—the proven, perfect car.

DESCRIPTION
Model "C" 1911

Motor—Westinghouse, special four-pole series. The largest used on any pleasure vehicle.
Transmission—From motor to counter-shaft by silent chain, running in oil and enclosed in dust-proof aluminum case.
Drive—Double chain system. The roller chains are run in aluminum cases which are absolutely noiseless, of the greatest efficiency and lifelong durability.
Controller—Continuous, torque, drum type. Forward and reverse in one handle. You have complete control of the car at all times.
Speeds—Four, forward to 19 miles per hour, all in one handle. There is no resistance coil. The car can be run on any of the four speeds without loss of current.
Bearings—Timken bearings in front and rear axles; German bearings in counter-shaft and motor.
Steering—(Left) side lever.
Wheel Base—78 inches.
Gauge—Standard 56 inches.
Wheels—Swartz artillery type, 34 inches, 12 spokes, 1½ inch.
Tires—34 x 4 rear and front. Either Motz cushion, or choice of pneumatic.
Brakes—Powerful internal expanding in rear hubs. Motor brake by backward movement of controller handle.
Springs—Highest grade steel, especially tempered, full elliptic rear; semi-elliptic front.
Batteries—Exide, 24 cells, 11 M. V. or Edison.
Mileage—65 to 70 mile.
Color—Maroon, dark blue, Brewster green.
Upholstery—Best French goat skin to match finish.
Sangson Ammeter, with automatic cut-out, which eliminates all risk of overcharging and spoiling the batteries.
Yale Lock Switch (insures safety). Current cannot be turned on without the key. This special device, with a complete system of locks for windows and doors, makes the car burglar proof.
Equipment—Two side lamps and tail light, complete toilet case; Jones Speedometer and Cyclometer.
Special color and trimmings without extra charge.

Write for the Catalogue

A few desirable agencies are still open

Phipps - Grinnell Auto Company

12-14 East Atwater Street Detroit, Michigan

The 1911 Phipps-Grinnell Model C, one of the first to offer a key-lock switch. The Phipps-Grinnell was also equipped with an enclosed chain drive. Note the contrast between the Phipps-Grinnell and the Borland ads. Phipps-Grinnell extols the virtues of chain drive and pedal-controlled reversing while Borland attacks these features as primitive and touts its own shaft drive and controls as the ultimate.

The Only Electric Car That Has A Two-Speed Planetary Transmission

You will realize immediately what that means.

You know what a handicap your gas car would be under if it was forced to operate exclusively on high gear.

Yet the Church-Field is the only car that eliminates that handicap in the electric field.

The Church-Field has both a high and a low gear.

It thus combines, for the first time, all the simplicity of control, the economy and convenience of the electric, with the power, reliability, and general efficiency of the gasoline car.

The Church-Field Electric Automobile marks a new era in electrically driven vehicles.

Here, at last, is an electric car that retains all the characteristics and advantages of its type and yet possesses that ability to do things—that sturdy utility that has hitherto belonged exclusively to the gasoline car.

Church-Field Electric

is not an experiment—for three years it has stood the test of hard, constant usage, under most trying conditions.

The superior advantages of its exclusive features have been demonstrated beyond question.

And these exclusive advantages include, in addition to the two-speed transmission, the Church-Field ten-point speed control—giving extreme flexibility.

The Church-Field safety locking and interlocking devices on the control lever.

The Church-Field reverse, three-quarter elliptic springs.

And a multitude of smaller refinements and conveniences that contribute materially to the luxury and efficiency of the car.

The Church-Field is the electric you have been waiting for.

A demonstration will convince you.

Write to-day for the beautifully illustrated catalogue and the name of nearest dealer.

Church-Field Motor Company, Sibley, Mich.

The 1913 Church-Field enclosed sedan and roadster. Note that the enclosed car houses a cozy group of ladies chatting, while the open vehicle is presented as more of a "man's car." The planetary transmission is basically a large "sun" gear in mesh with smaller "planet" gears.

not compete. Oil was cheap in the first half of the century, cheap enough to make operating a gasoline car less expensive than running an electric car in most places. After Henry Ford began to produce his Model T, gasoline cars became available to almost everybody. A new Model T could be had for five hundred dollars in 1915. At the same time, electric cars were priced in the thousands.

The slow speed of electric cars also contributed to their demise. Electric cars boasted a top speed of 20 to 30 miles per hour. By 1915 gasoline cars were available that could top 100 miles per hour. However, most traveled comfortably around 40 miles per hour, if the road allowed. But even 40 miles per hour was much better than any electric car could hope to achieve. Cars with roaring gasoline engines were considered "manly" machines, while electric cars had a definite feminine association.

As one might expect, as soon as there were two self-propelled vehicles that could travel more than a few feet at a time, there were races. From around 1900 to 1910 a series of well-publicized races solidified the position of the gasoline engine as the one to use if you wanted speed. Almost all of these races were won by gasoline-engine-powered cars. Steam cars won some, but few electric cars could even come close to winning. However, electric cars did demonstrate their dependability. Most cars in these early races never finished. They broke down. Some gasoline cars literally blew apart during races. Electric cars tended to keep going, but only as long as their batteries held out. Other contestants were not about to wait around politely for eight hours or so while the batteries were recharged. Nor did electric-car drivers have to wait; race crews made sure that a supply of fresh batteries was on hand.

But not everyone could have fresh batteries brought to them by a pit crew. Here was a factor in the electric car's failure. As pointed out earlier, the primary reason for owning an automobile was the freedom it gave you to go where you wanted to go when you wanted to go there. The electric car could go only where there was electricity to recharge the batteries. In the early part of the century, most of the rural United States did not have electricity. In fact, it was not until the 1940s that most of rural America was "electrified." And it was the people in the country who really needed automobiles. There were trolley cars and trains in the cities. But in the country you had to use horses, your own muscles, or gasoline or steam automobiles.

It is true that gasoline filling stations were also rare in rural America in the 1900s and 1910s. Owning an automobile, however, meant also owning the means to keep it supplied with fuel. A farmer with an automobile was able to strap a hundred-gallon drum to his car and drive to the nearest gasoline station, fill up the drum, and store the fuel on the farm. Gasoline could be stored. Electricity could not.

Ironically, an electrical device hastened the electric car's departure. This device was the electric self-starter which ended the need for cranking gasoline engines. A starter is an electric motor that turns the engine until it fires or "turns over." The electric starter removed one of the last barriers between women and complete driving freedom. No longer did a woman have to depend on a strong-armed man to start a gasoline car. The lady could start the car herself by stepping on or pushing a switch; this was almost as easy as starting an electric car. There was no longer any reason for women to limit themselves to electric cars.

The situation today is quite different than it was in the 1910s. Gasoline is no longer cheap, and we know that the supply of petroleum will not last forever. Electricity is available just about everywhere in the country. The times would seem opportune for a comeback for the electric car.

There are, however, many technical, economic, and other problems to solve if electric vehicles are ever again to become a major means of transportation. And foremost among these problems is a reliable source of electrical energy.

2

A SOURCE OF ENERGY

It may not always be obvious, but nothing moves without energy. Even coasting down a hill requires energy, the energy of gravity. Living things need the energy contained in food. Food is fuel to a living thing. Of course, the burning of fuel in a plant or an animal is not quite the same as what happens in a gasoline engine. There is no flame and explosion in a living thing, but there is release of energy from the food fuel and much of that energy is heat energy. The similarity is in the basic process of oxidation—that is, the combining of fuel with oxygen. When this oxidation occurs fairly rapidly, as in the combining of oxygen with a fireplace log, there is flame. When the oxidation is even more rapid, as in the combining of gasoline with oxygen in a gasoline engine, the result can be an explosion.

What about an energy source for an electric car? Obviously, the energy needed to run an electric car is electricity. But where does the electricity come from? For many people, the knowledge of the source of electricity does not go beyond the wall plug. If you want to run an electrical appliance you plug it in. If you want lights you flip on a switch. Jokesters have suggested a "long extension cord" for electric cars. That possibility is not entirely a joke. It is entirely possible that some day electric cars might be run from a central power source much as electric trains and trolley cars are.

For the present, however, electric cars cannot be "plugged in" while they are running. The source of power must be carried with them. The word that immediately comes to mind is "battery." The power source for an electric car may indeed be a battery. Most electric cars available today, including golf carts and electric forklifts, carry batteries. In the future, however, there may be electric cars that run on devices that cannot strictly be called batteries. Whatever they may be called, portable power sources for electric cars will have one thing in common and that is, they will produce electricity through chemical reactions.

No discussion of electricity is possible without using the terms *amperes*, *volts*, and *watts*. These are units of electrical measurements. They are also widely misunderstood.

Electricity as a term also defies definition. An electric current can be defined as a "flow of electrons." A flow of electrons is indeed what an electric current is. "Current," as a term,

The Vanguard, made by Vanguard Motors, Kingston, New York. Designed for city and off-road use, the manufacturers claim 40–60 miles on a charge, depending on temperature and terrain. The maximum claimed speed is 28 miles per hour. The body is made of fiberglass and the frame is aluminum. It runs on six 6-volt batteries. Its single-speed transmission is through a double-reduction-gear drive. (*Vanguard Motors*)

implies movement, such as a river current. But saying that electricity is a flow or current of electrons does not tell us how electricity does useful things such as making light bulbs glow, electric stoves heat, and electric motors move. For the moment, it is sufficient to know that the flow of electrons that is electricity is a form of energy that can be converted to other forms of energy, such as light, heat, and motion.

An electron can be thought of as a unit of electrical "charge." But an electron is too small an entity to work with conveniently. The ampere, then, is the standard unit of current.

It is defined as 6.24×10^{18} electrons passing a given point a second. 6.24×10^{18} is a ridiculously huge number (6,240,000,-000,000,000,000) which, if nothing else, helps to get across the idea of how small an electron is.

The volt is often referred to as the "unit of electrical pressure," that is, the force that "pushes" electrons, though this common attempt to define it is not entirely accurate. The volt is a measure of the source of the electrical energy. The source can be a cell or an electrical generator. Another way of defining the volt is "the standard unit of energy per unit of electric charge."

The watt is a measurement of electrical power. It can be directly related to horsepower (746 watts = one horsepower). The number of watts indicated on a light bulb is not a measure of how bright the bulb is. Rather it is a measure of how much energy the bulb uses in a given amount of time. Watts can also be expressed in terms of volts and amperes:

$$\text{watts (power)} = \text{volts (energy per unit charge)} \times \text{amperes (charges per second)}$$

A current of electricity can move in one direction or it can alternate. Current that moves in one direction is called direct current (DC). Cells produce direct current. Most generators are made to produce alternating current (AC). That is, the current reverses directions. How many direction changes take place each minute depends on the speed of the generator.

The "batteries" that are put into flashlights, toys, transistor radios, and so on are not batteries in the strict sense of the word. They are cells, which produce electricity through chemical reactions.

The word battery means a collection or a group. All batteries are made up of combinations of cells. The cell is the basic unit. Simply speaking, a cell is composed of any two different metals in a chemical solution called an electrolyte. Chemical action between the electrolyte and the metals produces electricity.

There are two kinds of cells that go to make up common batteries. They are called *primary* and *secondary*. Primary cells are the "basic" kind such as those used in flashlights. To produce electricity from them, all that is needed is the two metals placed separately in the electrolyte solution. When an outside "load"—a light bulb, motor, or anything else electricity can activate—is connected between the two metals, chemical reactions will begin immediately producing a flow of electrons—an electric current.

When a primary cell is used, energy is taken out of it to do work. The energy is in the electric current, but it comes from the chemical reactions going on in the cell. (In a similar way, the energy in the heat of a match comes out of the chemical reactions going on in the burning match head.)

The "electrolyte" can be practically any water solution that will conduct electricity well. It can be a solution of an acid, an alkali, or a salt (even table salt). If a primary cell such as a flashlight cell is taken apart, the electrolyte will not look like a solution at all. It will appear to be solid, but it is "wet" enough, that is moist, for the necessary chemical reactions to take place.

You could just stick a strip of copper and a strip of zinc into a lemon, and you would get electricity out of that. The lemon juice is slightly acid and will serve as an electrolyte. Of course, some combinations of metals and electrolytes work better than others. But almost any combination will produce some electricity.

You could even use potatoes. Three or four small potatoes, each with a strip of copper and a strip of zinc, can be connected together to light a penlight bulb to full brilliance. Each potato can then be thought of as a cell, and all the potato "cells" connected together can be thought of as a battery.

All cells have a positive terminal (or electrode) and a negative terminal. In a flashlight cell the positive terminal is the little button at one end of the cell. The negative terminal is usually at the end opposite from the positive terminal. The electricity flows from the negative terminal through the load and back into the cell through the positive terminal. Inside the cell the flow of current is from positive to negative.

Batteries of secondary cells are used in automobiles to provide electricity for starting and ignition. These cells are rechargeable. At the present time, secondary cells of one kind or another are used in electric cars. Because they are charged by having electricity run through them, there is the impression that the battery is being "filled" with electricity and that the electricity is being stored. For that reason they are called "storage batteries." Of course, electricity is not being stored. When a car battery is charged, energy is indeed stored, but not as electricity. The energy goes into the battery as electricity and comes out as electricity, but it is stored as chemical energy.

The electricity sent into the battery causes certain chemical changes to occur. These changes serve to store energy. When the energy is used, a new set of chemical reactions takes place. These reactions release electrons, which flow through the load outside the battery as electricity. Sending electricity into the battery is called charging. When electricity from the battery is used, the battery is discharged.

Most of the secondary-cell batteries in use today are the lead-acid type. The negative terminal is made of pure lead. The positive terminal is made of *lead oxide*. These are two different materials. The electrolyte will act on them in different ways.

The electrolyte is a common acid—sulfuric acid—in some water. This acid can react with metals to form compounds called *sulfates*. While a lead-acid cell or battery is being used, lead sulfate forms. This means that lead and acid are both chemically changed. Three major chemical things happen as the cell is discharged. The acid gets weaker, water is formed, and lead sulfate is deposited on all plates. This coating of lead sulfate prevents acid from touching the remaining lead and lead oxide. The reactions that are producing electricity—and lead sulfate—get weaker and weaker. If this were a primary cell, eventually all useful reactions would stop.

However, if an electric current is passed through the lead-acid cell in the "reverse" direction, the cell is all but rebuilt. Lead sulfate breaks down. It becomes lead and sulfate ions. Some lead returns to the negative electrode—that is, the all-lead plate. Not only that, but the water that was formed in the discharging reaction breaks down. The water becomes hydrogen and oxygen ions. The oxygen combines with lead, making lead oxide. This new lead oxide is deposited on the lead oxide plate. The hydrogen ions left over from the breakdown of water now "balance" the sulfate ions that were set free when lead sulfate was broken down. This "balanced" collection of hydrogen and sulfate ions in a water solution is sulfuric acid.

Now there is a renewed lead plate, a renewed lead oxide plate, and a renewed solution of sulfuric acid. It took energy to accomplish all this. Some of that energy has been stored in the cell's chemical system. If a load is hooked up once more, so that electrons can leave the negative terminal, lead from the negative plate will start dissolving in the acid. The whole "discharge" process starts again.

Electricity enters and leaves a storage battery through the two terminals or posts on the outside of the case that encloses the cells. The positive terminal and the negative terminal are connected to the positive and negative cells respectively. The "discharge" or electricity-producing reactions take place when the battery is connected to a load. This is usually done with wires leading from the terminals.

Cells are arranged in batteries to increase the voltage or to increase the amount of current. If the positive terminal of one cell is connected to the negative terminal of another, the result is a two-cell battery. This battery has double the voltage of a single cell—and, like a cell, still has a positive and a negative terminal. These are the "leftover" terminals that were not connected together. They can be connected to a load to do work.

More cells can be added—positive to negative to positive to negative and so on. The voltage of each cell is added to the battery. Thus, a battery of four 1.5-volt cells would have a total of 6 volts. This arrangement is one of two possible ways to connect cells. It is called a *series* connection. It results in an increase of voltage from the battery, but the amount of *current* that can be drawn at any one time remains the same as for one cell.

The other way to connect cells is in *parallel*. The negative terminals of all cells are connected together, and the positive terminals of all the cells are connected together. The number of cells does not matter. The load is still connected between positive and negative terminals as before. It does not matter where the load connections are made—at the "first cell" or the "last cell" or somewhere in the middle. It is as if the battery had one big negative terminal and one big positive terminal.

In this parallel arrangement, the voltage does not increase. It will be the same as for one cell. But the amount of current available is twice, three times, four times—x times the amount from one cell, x being the total number of cells.

Batteries are almost always manufactured with the *series* connection. If a high current capacity is needed, then several entire series-connected batteries may be connected in parallel. Entire batteries can be connected as if they were cells. In principle, any voltage and any current rating can be achieved by series and parallel connections.

The energy output of a battery of secondary cells varies with temperature and the rate of current discharge. In general, the colder the temperature, the less efficient the battery is. The temperature effect is one reason why gasoline cars with old batteries sometimes don't get started on cold mornings.

Cells and batteries are usually rated in terms of "amperehours," a value that is obtained by multiplying the discharge rate in amperes times the hours of discharge. So, if a battery can give four amperes for twenty hours, its rating is 80 amperehours. There are other rating units such as the watt-pound, which is the energy in watts obtainable per pound of battery. The weight of the battery is, of course, an important consideration in electric-car applications.

As mentioned before, the lead-acid is not the only kind of secondary or "storage" cell. Some other types are candidates for the powering of electric cars. They work the same way as lead-acid cells—that is, they involve chemical reactions that can be *reversed*. There are also some other interesting possibilities that work on principles that are somewhat different. The most highly perfected of these is the fuel cell.

The general idea of *any* kind of cell is two different electrodes in some kind of electrolyte. Chemical action between the electrodes and the electrolyte converts stored chemical energy into electrical energy. Fuel cells still have an electrolyte of some kind. Instead of having two metals as electrodes, however, they have a *fuel* and an *oxidizer*.

The idea of combining a fuel with an oxidizer to get energy is nothing new. This is what is done when a stick of wood or a candle or a piece of coal or a drop of oil or a puff of cooking gas is burned. These fuels are combined with oxygen and the energy released is heat and often light. In the fuel cell, electricity, not heat, is the form of energy released.

The idea of getting electricity out of a fuel and oxygen is not new either. It was suggested early in the nineteenth century. It was tried in the laboratory and it worked. At least it worked well enough to show that it could be done. But there were not many practical uses for electricity before the telegraph came into use. (That was not until 1845, when Samuel F. B. Morse founded a company.) By that time, primary cells worked very well. Not many years later, good secondary cells were available. By the last quarter of the nineteenth century, good direct-current (DC) generators were in use. Progress had passed the fuel cell by. No one wanted to take the trouble to develop it.

The fuel cell idea never really died. But it took the space program to get it out of hibernation. Large amounts of power, from a reliable source and with good weight economy, were needed for manned space capsules. Development was rapid. From what was nearly a standing start, fuel cells were developed for the Project Gemini spacecraft (the Geminis carried two men each). In a few more years, fuel cells supplied electric power for the three-man Project Apollo moon-flight missions.

The Gemini and Apollo programs used one of the simpler types of fuel cell systems. Pure hydrogen is the fuel. Pure oxygen is the oxidizer. The by-product is pure water—a useful dividend on a spaceship.

How can electricity be obtained from the combination of hydrogen and oxygen? The usual release of energy from this reaction is in the form of heat, not electricity. The simplest way to combine the two gases involves applying some heat—a flame or a spark. Then the hydrogen burns; that is, it combines with oxygen, producing an extremely high temperature. In fact, very rapid combustion or explosion is a serious risk.

In the Project Apollo fuel cells, the two gases do not combine by direct burning. They combine through chemical action with the electrolyte. The electrolyte contains a *catalyst* to enable the reaction to proceed at a low temperature. (A catalyst is an element or chemical that speeds up a chemical reaction without being consumed or changed in the reaction.) *All* chemical reactions of this type involve exchanges of electrons between the atoms. The burning of hydrogen with oxygen to produce heat is no exception. In burning, however, the electron exchange is too

The Lead Wedge Special holds the world's speed record for electric cars. The car achieved a speed of 138.8 miles per hour on the Bonneville Salt Flats in 1973. The car was built and run as a promotion for the Autolite battery made by the Ford Motor Company. With the fiberglass body off, the position of the driver and batteries can be seen. (*Ford Motor Company*)

In a car similar to the Lead Wedge, Mickey Thompson races across the Bonneville Salt Flats. (*Ford Motor Company*)

direct and too fast to be useful as a source of electric current. But when slowed down and controlled by means of the electrolyte, this exchange can take place through a path outside the cell. The result is a stream of electrons in a wire or circuit. Energy in the form of electricity can be tapped from this stream of electrons.

Of course, the designers of these fuel cells had a great deal to think about. Their hydrogen-oxygen cells were simple *in principle*. But to get them built and make them work was not at all like sticking two pieces of metal into a lemon or a potato. Their "simple" cell is not crude. It is an engineering marvel.

The "electrodes" are two hollow chambers made of metal, so they will conduct electricity. Oxygen gas fills one chamber, hydrogen gas the other. Methods of handling the gases in the vacuum of space had to be devised. This was only one of many problems solved by the fuel cell designers.

The electrolyte had to be a liquid. Somehow, both gases had to be brought into contact with the electrolyte, without the gases mixing. So, a porous electrolyte-holder was made, something like a sponge. Only it had to be rigid and strong, able to withstand pressures. The material chosen was a ceramic, like porcelain. The electrolyte-holder acted as a wall to separate the two electrode chambers.

The sleek, sporty Sundancer is an experimental electric car designed by the Electric Storage Battery Company. It was made as a test for the company's lead-acid batteries. Equipped with twelve 6-volt lead-acid batteries and an 8-horsepower motor, the car can go as fast as 60 miles per hour. It has a two-speed manual transmission and disk brakes. The seven-step contactor controller provides a typical range of voltage controls. Four steps are at half voltage with the two halves of the battery connected in parallel. Three steps are connected in series at full voltage. The controller is an experimental device that serves both as power controller and battery charger. (*Electric Storage Battery Company*)

The by-product, water vapor, also presented a problem. Somehow, the water vapor had to be continuously removed from the cell. Water vapor is a gas. It had to be removed without also removing the hydrogen or oxygen or both. One possibility was to condense the water vapor into liquid water. But since the vehicle was to go into space, the resulting weightlessness could make getting the water out difficult. It could not be expected to "flow down" and out of the cell. Even in an earthbound situation it could be difficult to get liquid water out without having to take the electrolyte out along with it. Through the use of some very sophisticated and very expensive technology, these problems were all solved. Hydrogen-oxygen fuel cells proved to be very valuable in the space program, although one of them exploded in Apollo 13.

Hydrogen and oxygen are carried in *liquid* form in spacecraft to save bulk. Hydrogen would also have to be carried in liquid form in an electric car powered by fuel cells. The oxygen can be taken from the air surrounding the car. But carrying a gas in liquid form requires low temperature, high pressure, *or both*. In the case of hydrogen, it is both. The need for liquid hydrogen is one reason why the Project Apollo fuel cell idea has not been used to any great extent for electric cars. This is not to say that liquid hydrogen will never be part of electric car technology. But it is an expensive and potentially dangerous approach right now.

A battery of hydrogen-oxygen cells may be too expensive for an electric car. Even if the cells are fairly cheap to make, the container for the hydrogen would be expensive. It has to be somewhat like an armored thermos bottle. It must be constructed in such a way that it will be strong enough not to burst from the pressure of the gas. The structure must also keep the temperature down. The liquefied hydrogen gas itself is also expensive.

However, other fuel cells are possible. Some manufacturers are trying to develop a kerosene cell. Kerosene is a *hydrocarbon*. It is a compound of hydrogen and carbon. Either element makes a good fuel for a fuel cell (although pure hydrogen is best in terms of energy per pound). Gasoline is another hydrocarbon. There are many cheap hydrocarbons. Methods of storing them and carrying them in relatively cheap tanks are well known. The technology of feeding them to the engine, furnace, or other energy-conversion device is also well developed.

The idea of a kerosene or gasoline fuel cell for an electric car seems somewhat startling. One of the main reasons for having electric cars is to reduce air pollution, or even to prevent it entirely. It would seem that using hydrocarbons in fuel cells would produce air pollution. One of the polluting exhaust vapors of a gasoline engine is sulfur dioxide. This is because there is sulfur in the gasoline. In the cylinders of the engine, sulfur combines with oxygen from the air. Perhaps sulfur dioxide would not be produced by a fuel cell. The sulfur might not react with the electrolyte. Or the sulfur products might be liquids that would stay in the fuel cell system (until drained by a mechanic). If only the hydrogen and carbon in the kerosene or gasoline are "used" by a fuel cell, the main exhaust products will be carbon dioxide and water vapor.

One type of fuel cell under development is called the "zinc-air battery." This is a battery made up of fuel cells that use zinc metal as fuel. The oxidizer is oxygen from the air. The products of the cells are electricity and zinc oxide. The latter is a solid material. The cell could be constructed so that the zinc oxide would collect inside the battery rather than being exhausted into the air.

The servicing routine for such a battery would include removing the zinc oxide "ash," as well as adding new zinc powder. Developers of the zinc oxide fuel cell battery claim that the zinc oxide could easily be recycled. This would probably have to be done in factories, not in the batteries. But recycling prevents waste as well as pollution.

Just as there are many combinations of materials that will make primary cells—some good, some poor—there are many ways to make a storage battery. Storage batteries are made with alkaline as well as acid electrolytes. A variety of metals and metal compounds can be used for electrodes. Among the possible combinations are nickel and iron, nickel and cadmium, cadmium and silver oxide, and zinc and silver oxide. (The latter two are usually nicknamed "silver-cadmium" and "silver-zinc" respectively.)

All of these types of batteries tend to be more expensive than the lead-acid battery, but they have certain advantages. One quality sought after in batteries is *energy density*. It is the amount of energy that can be delivered per pound of battery weight. Energy density is usually expressed in "watt-hours per pound." This is important for an electric car—the lighter the power source, the better.

The following table is a compilation of information about different kinds of storage batteries. There are many ways of figuring energy density, and engineers often disagree. This table is designed only to give you a rough idea of how batteries compare.

At the right-hand side of the table is a column for relative cost. A silver-zinc or silver-cadmium battery, for example, costs ten times as much as a lead-acid battery of the same rating.

Battery Type	Energy Density (Watt-hours per pound)	Relative Cost
Lead-Acid	8 to 12	$ 1
Nickel-Iron	11	3
Nickel-Cadmium	12 to 14	6
Silver-Zinc	40 to 60	10
Silver-Cadmium	30	10

According to the table, silver zinc looks good: expensive, but with plenty of power per pound. There are, however, other things to consider, such as the operating life of the battery.

What are some of the things that affect the operating life of a battery? A very important consideration is how many complete charge-discharge cycles it can take. An electric car running its full range every day will completely discharge its batteries every day. Of course, most electric cars probably will not be driven that far every day and so would not completely discharge their batteries every day. But still, the number of partial charge-discharge cycles must be related to the "whole cycle" number in some way. Whatever kind of battery is used in an electric car, the complete set is going to be expensive. The buyer would want them to last a long time. So, another table:

Battery Type	Life in Operating Cycles (Maximum)	Relative Cost
Lead-Acid	400	$ 1
Nickel-Iron	3,000	3
Nickel-Cadmium	2,000	6
Silver-Zinc	300	10
Silver-Cadmium	3,000	10

Now, that silver-zinc battery does not look quite so good. It is "best" from the energy-density standpoint. But it has a short operating life—only three hundred cycles. Is it even as good as the best lead-acid batteries?

How about silver cadmium? It has an energy density of about 30 watt-hours per pound, which is between three and four times as good as a lead-acid battery. It still has ten times the cost.

A typical price for a lead-acid car battery is forty dollars. From this figure and the data in the tables, you can compute that the cost of a silver-cadmium battery of the same rating would be four hundred dollars. Four hundred dollars seems a small price to pay for a battery that can be recharged three thousand times. But four hundred dollars for one battery is neither the full need nor the full price. One battery is not enough for an electric car. The forty-dollar lead-acid battery in a gasoline car *does not propel the whole car*. Its main purpose is starting the car. For most gasoline cars, a battery with 12 volts and 30 or 40 ampere-hours is more than enough.

A battery of 12 volts and only 30 or 40 ampere-hours capacity is not enough to run an electric car. Such a battery multiplies out to 180 to 240 watts of power, for one hour of discharge. But one horsepower equals 746 watts. An electric car will need something between 20 and 50 horsepower—that is, between 15,000 and 37,000 watts—and will need it for more

Many people have made their own electric cars or have converted conventional cars. Shown here is a converted Volkswagen Kharman Ghia. The electric motor is in the back, the same place the Kharman Ghia's gasoline engine used to be. The conversion was made by Thomas Thiele, an engineer at the Allis-Chalmers Company. Thirty 12-volt batteries are jammed under the front hood and under the seats. The 27-horsepower motor was originally designed as a ground power generator for auxiliary power to start aircraft. The motor delivers power to the wheels through a regular Volkswagen four-speed transmission.

The builder claims a top speed of 75 miles per hour and the ability to go an hour at 60 miles per hour on one charge. The engineer was assisted in his car-building efforts by Allis-Chalmers. (*Allis-Chalmers Company*) than one hour. That kind of output is roughly equivalent to the output of 60 to 150 "regular" lead-acid car batteries. At ten times the cost *per unit*, the total cost comes to 600 to 1,500 times the cost of one gasoline car battery. The cheapest silver-cadmium battery for an all-electric car will cost thousands of dollars.

Engineers and auto-builders have pointed out that silver-electrode batteries may inspire a new kind of thief—someone who steals batteries instead of whole cars or who steals cars to get the batteries, for the silver in them. Of course, the battery "pack" for an electric car would be very bulky and heavy. So would a single battery. And getting the silver out of the batteries would be some job. But it is something to think about.

Silver is in short supply. Several years ago the United States switched from silver dimes, quarters, and half dollars to sandwich coins. These have a copper base with silver-alloy facings on both sides. It is no simple matter to go out and mine more silver. It happens that silver is one of the world's most badly depleted resources. Over time, new silver will probably get scarcer and scarcer, and more expensive.

Still, some companies in the electric-car field are pushing for silver batteries. The suggestion has been made that such batteries be rented, not purchased, by the user of the car. This would reduce the car owner's expense and risk. Something of this nature could probably be worked out. Plans for renting electric cars have been successful in some cities.

Of course, the silver in a battery would never be used up. Not even once the battery was dead, at the end of its service life. The silver would still be there; it could be recycled. Given its scarcity, manufacturers would be eager to recycle it. This is one reason for rent-a-battery plans. The manufacturer wants to be sure he will get the silver back for recycling. The best way to insure that is for him to own the battery wherever it goes.

So, while some disadvantages have been mentioned here—

mainly the expense—silver-cadmium and perhaps silver-zinc batteries are definitely in the running.

One disadvantage, possibly a slight one, of all other batteries compared to the lead-acid type is low cell voltage. Lead-acid cells are rated at 2 volts. The lead-acid cell's 2 volts may drop to about 1.5 volts under heavy discharge. But most of the others only give 1.3 volts under light discharge and perhaps 0.75 volt under heavy discharge.

Available power depends on voltage and current. A heavy load tends to draw a heavy current. If voltage drops too much, not as much current can be delivered. Also, the easiest way to get high power is to have a high voltage and to let the load draw a smaller current. This is easier on the battery system for many reasons. But if cell voltages are low to begin with, this means using more cells per battery. Using more cells means more headaches for the designer and the manufacturer. It also means more cells to service during use.

For this reason, as well as cheapness, the old lead-acid battery is holding its own. Golf carts, industrial forklifts, and other low-speed, short-range electric utility cars are powered by it. Some experts think that when all is said and done, the family electric car may yet be powered by it.

Some electric-car developers are considering using more than one kind of battery in a combination or "hybrid" pack. This might enable a designer to take advantage of the best points of more than one kind of battery. For example, a silver-zinc system might supply heavy currents for starting, accelerating, or going uphill. But a nickel-iron system might take over for steady cruising. This would take advantage of the high power density of silver-zinc, and the lower cost and many recharge cycles of nickel-iron.

One or two manufacturers are experimenting with hybrid power packages that use both fuel cells (such as zinc-air) and storage batteries (even lead-acid).

The Electra King, made by B and Z Electric Car, Long Beach, California, is available in three-wheel and four-wheel models. The tricycle model is a nimble vehicle with a twelve-foot turning circle. It can be equipped with hand or foot controls. Powered by six 6-volt batteries, it cruises at 20 miles per hour and gets up to forty miles on a charge. (*B and Z Electric Car*)

Another hybrid idea is using a small gasoline engine to provide part of the power, and an electric motor and smaller-sized battery system to provide the other part. This seems to be a promising approach, and indeed it has been done. But this mechanical arrangement has its own set of problems. The idea is being worked on however.

The problems discussed in this chapter are not so severe that electric cars cannot be built. Nor do the problems neces-

sarily imply that electric cars will be too expensive to compete
with other forms of transportation. These present problems are
only the reasons why the streets are not swarming with quiet,
efficient, nonpolluting "electrics" right now. Development work
remains to be done. This will take time, money, and faith on the
part of manufacturers and potential buyers.

3

HOW DOES AN
ELECTRIC MOTOR WORK?

An electric motor converts electrical energy into mechanical energy. The electrical energy is in that mysterious stuff, electricity, flowing in its wires. The mechanical energy shows up as movement in the motor. "Mechanical energy" is another way of saying motion or moving. The moving part of the motor is attached to a rotating shaft, which can be hooked up to transfer the motion to a vehicle or other device. The electrical energy can come from a power socket in the kitchen wall, or from a battery. Motors can run on AC (alternating current) or DC (direct current). There are motors that will run only on AC or only on DC, but the operating principle is the same in both. The two kinds of motors differ only in the ways in which the principle is applied.

In fact, many small motors (around ⅛ horsepower) are called *universal* motors because their design permits them to run on either kind of current. However, given its particular design, a universal motor will run better on one type of current than the other. For larger horsepower ratings, engineers design a motor to run either on AC or DC, not both. It seldom if ever happens that versatility is needed in a very large motor. The engineer designs for best performance on one kind of current, and saves the customer a lot of expensive overdesign. The most common kind of AC motor, called the induction motor, cannot run on DC at all. It will give a sort of starting jolt, then stop and sit there getting hotter and hotter until a fuse blows somewhere.

The choice of motor for an electric car is not an easy one to make. Batteries produce DC, so it would seem that all that needs to be done is to design an efficient DC motor for use in electric cars. However, there are plans for electric cars to use "mains" power in cities. Main power is AC. Therefore electric-car motors may need to be "universal." If so, they can be. But an electric-car motor must be hefty, not just ⅛ horsepower. If it is both universal and hefty, it is going to be tricky to design —and expensive.

An engineer will often sacrifice versatility for best performance. There are, for example, many cheap, squawky little kitchen radios that feature AC/DC operation. But no fine, high fidelity stereo system or really good tape recorder is AC/DC. In *theory*, a gasoline engine could run on kerosene, alcohol, natu-

The DELTA is an experimental electric car from General Electric. DELTA is an acronym for Developmental Electric Town Auto. It is equipped with two battery systems. The main battery is a 72-volt experimental lead-acid battery, rated at 225 amp-hours. The car also has a 72-volt, 11-amp-hour nickel-cadmium vented battery that is used as an acceleration booster. The acceleration-booster battery is capable of a very high discharge rate. The circuit automatically increases the current delivery from the nickel-cadmium battery as the load increases beyond the economical capability of the main battery. The booster battery is automatically recharged from the main battery.

The DELTA has a top speed of 55 miles per hour. Its range is about 110 miles at 30 miles per hour and fifty to sixty miles at 40 miles per hour. It has a station-wagon-type door at the back. (*General Electric Company*) ral gas—just about any fluid that has carbon and hydrogen available for burning. In fact, converting a gasoline engine for natural gas is fairly easy, and it simplifies the engine. There is no need for a complex carburetor. But it would be necessary to change spark plug gaps, fool with the timing, worry about compression, and perhaps sacrifice some performance. What's more, gasoline engines come in different designs: for high-octane fuel, lower-octane fuel, leaded or unleaded fuel, and so on.

It is easier and cheaper all around to design a heat engine to run on one kind of fuel. In theory, it is possible to build an engine that would switch from fuel to fuel at the turn of a knob. But it would be expensive. The same goes for electric motors. In theory, and even in practice, electric motors can run on AC, DC, or both; on high voltage, low voltage, or both; and so on. But if the design options increase, the cost increases.

Whatever the design of an electric motor, they all operate on the same principle—magnetic attraction and repulsion. Any magnet has two *poles*, respectively called a "north-seeking pole" and a "south-seeking pole." It is well known that if the north-seeking (or N) pole of one magnet is brought near the south-seeking (S) pole of another, the magnets will pull toward each other strongly. If the N (or S) pole of one of the magnets is brought toward the *middle* of the other magnet, a weak pull is felt. It is no stronger than the pull between a magnet and an ordinary piece of iron or steel.

What happens if the N pole of one magnet is brought near the N pole of the other? They seem to push apart. This repulsion can be felt if an attempt is made to bring the magnets together. If the magnets are heavy and strong, it is quite a job to get two N poles (or two S poles) to touch at all. In some instances, it is practically impossible.

A compass can also be used to demonstrate magnetic attraction and repulsion. The compass "needle" itself is a small magnet, of course, just a lightweight bar magnet suspended on a pivot at its center. Bring one pole of any kind of magnet near it, and one end of the compass needle snaps over to point toward that pole. By moving the magnet carefully in a circle, you can make that same end of the needle follow the magnet all the way around the circle. By leaving the magnet in place but turning the compass so that the other pole is near the magnet, you can make the compass needle shift abruptly the same way. The N pole of the magnet will attract the S pole of the compass, and vice versa. But the N pole will also repel the compass's N pole, push it away.

The magnet can be used to make the compass needle go around and around. But to do this, the magnet must be kept moving in some way. The needle's movements represent mechanical energy. The energy of motion—the movements of your hand—must be constantly supplied. Indeed, energy must be constantly supplied to an electric motor to keep it going, but that energy is in the form of electricity, not the energy of motion. Even so, the movement of the compass needle shows a basic principle of the way electric motors work.

When electricity flows in a conductor (a wire), the conductor becomes a temporary magnet. That is, a magnetic field exists around the wire when electricity is passing through. When the electric current is turned off, the magnetic field collapses. The wire is no longer a magnet. But it can be again— just as soon as the current is turned on.

If the wire is bent into a loop, the wire's magnetic field is concentrated somewhat. The more wire and loops, the more concentrated the field is likely to be.

Suppose a loop is somehow suspended between the poles of a magnet. Suppose further that the magnet in Figure 1 is a horseshoe magnet, or a bar magnet bent in some way. Only the poles need to be considered, so the exact shape of the magnet

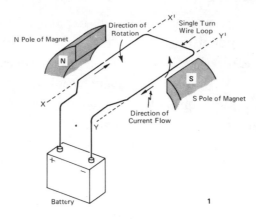

does not matter. The loop in the figure is drawn for simplicity rather than accuracy. Now suppose an electric current is fed through the left-hand end of the loop, the end marked "X." The current will go all the way through the loop, coming out the right-hand end, marked "Y." As it goes, it will cause a magnetic field to spring up all around the wire, something like a ghostly sleeve or coating on the wire. This field will have polarity, just as the magnet's does. The loop is a magnet.

As drawn here, with electric current going into the left-hand side of the loop, the loop's N pole is on the left. Since like poles repel, the two N poles will push away from each other. The magnet can be imagined as heavy and fixed; it will not move. So, the loop will move.

As drawn here, the left-hand side of the loop will move downward. That is, it will move counterclockwise.

To the right, exactly the same thing is happening, but the current is running the other way in the wire, and so the loop's S pole is on this side. But this part of the loop is near the S pole of the magnet. Again, all the forces here push the loop counterclockwise—the right-hand side of the loop moves upward.

How far does the loop move? Once this process gets started, the loop should flip over completely. The original left-

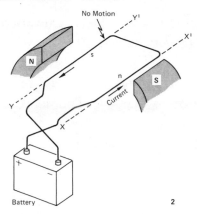

hand side (line X-X¹) will wind up near the magnet's S pole, and the original right-hand side (line Y-Y¹) will be near the N pole, as in Figure 2. This will happen provided the loop really is free to move. The loop will flip over once and then all movement will stop.

Why does movement stop? With the loop flipped, the current is now coming from the new left-hand side of the loop. It is still along line Y-Y¹, the S pole line for the loop. As long as the current keeps flowing that same way, it will remain the S pole. But the magnet's pole on the left is the N pole. Opposite poles attract. All the forces operating in this experiment now hold the Y-Y¹ part of the loop, its S pole, near the magnet's N pole. Needless to say, the loop segment, X-X¹, is still an N pole. It is now near the magnet's S pole. Unless something is done to change the situation, it will stay there.

What could be done to make the loop move again? Assume that the current is coming from a battery. Suppose the connections between the loop and the battery are switched. Whatever end of the loop had been connected to the positive terminal goes to the negative terminal, and vice versa. What happens?

The loop flips again. When the connections are switched,

the direction of current in the loop is reversed. Now current is *again* going into the left side of the loop and coming out on the right.

So the loop must flip again. It must make one more counterclockwise half-turn. And stop. The loop could be made to "go" once more by shifting battery connections again. Of course, shifting terminals by hand is hardly an efficient way to make something move.

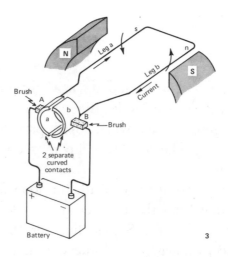

Suppose, however, current is fed to the loop through a pair of curved contacts as in Figure 3. These must be made of metal that conducts electricity. Assume they are copper, like the wire. Touching them are two *fixed* contacts called *brushes*. These could really be "brushes" of copper wire, say bundles of small wires, or they could be something softer and smoother. Most motors that have brushes (some do not) have brushes of graphite. This is a soft form of ordinary carbon. The brushes are connected to the battery, and the loop receives its current through the brushes and through the curved contacts. The curved contacts are free to rotate with the loop.

What happens when the current is turned on? The loop makes a half-turn, as before. But the moment it does, it reverses its connection with the battery. At first, brush A was touching rotating contact *a*. Brush B was touching contact *b*. But now the pairing is A*b* and B*a*.

Through most of the half-turn of flip, the side of the loop that was carrying current away from the battery, leg *a*, kept on carrying it that way. Through most of the flip, leg *a* of the loop was connected to the left brush, or brush A. Now leg *a* is connected to the right brush, or B. Now it must carry current toward the battery. The battery hasn't been touched, but the loop has reversed its connections. Every time the connections are reversed, the loop will move.

In a real motor, the loop would be attached to a shaft supported by bearings at its ends. The motion of the loop would continue for as long as the battery lasted. Given an "infinite" source of electricity, like a hydroelectric generator powered by some waterfall, the loop would continue to spin until the brushes or the bearings wore out. It would spin "indefinitely," though not quite forever.

Is this rotating loop really anything like a practical electric motor? Yes. There are motors whose *rotor* (the part that spins) consists of one "coil," which is often just one single-turn loop. This loop, however, will be a very heavy wire. For a great many reasons, it is usually better to have many turns of wire, and in fact, many separate coils. Imagine a two-coil motor with four rotating contacts and still two brushes. With this arrangement, it is possible to get smoother mechanical power out of the motor. But the motor could just as well have six or eight or ten or a hundred coils (or loops), with a pair of contact points for each, and deliver very smooth power.

The arrangement of contacts that feed the loops in a motor is called a *commutator*. This commutator reverses the current so that the rotor keeps turning. Every time the loop makes a half-turn (one flip), the direction of current reverses in the loop. The commutator keeps reversing the current so that

The Electrobus, manufactured by the Electrobus Company, Studio City, California, is a remarkably quiet public-transportation vehicle. It can be equipped with a variety of battery systems depending on just how it will be used. A typical battery is a 36-cell, 72-volt, 880-amp-hour, lead-acid single unit on a sliding tray. There is no transmission or gears, but rather a fully automatic speed control with an accelerator pedal.

The Electrobus has seating for twenty passengers. With a full load it can reach 35 miles per hour and climb a 25 per cent grade. (*Electrobus Company*)

the loop keeps on spinning. In any given segment of the wire, the current runs first in one direction, then in the opposite direction. Any current that reverses its direction in a regular way, as the loop current does, is an *alternating* current (AC). So, although the loop motor was fed from a battery, a DC source, the current in the loop is alternated.

Household AC in the United States completely reverses itself 60 times every second. That means there are 60 current pulses running in one direction every second, and 60 current pulses running in the opposite direction. That makes for 120 possible "power" pulses. Now, suppose our loop had the size, mass, and proper suspension to be able to do 120 "flips," or 60 complete turns, every second. The motor would not need a commutator, because each time the loop flipped over, the current coming into it would have reversed its direction just at the right time.

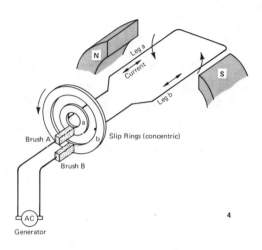

Although an AC motor need not use a commutator, current must somehow be fed to the spinning rotor. Again, brushes may be used, but this time they bear against a pair of slip rings, as shown in Figure 4. Each brush is always in contact, through its slip ring, with the same end of the loop. (With a commutator, each brush is connected to a different end on each half-turn.)

It is possible to feed current to a spinning rotor without using brushes or any other direct connection, provided the supply current is an alternating current. Energy can move through "empty space" from windings in the stationary part of the motor to the rotor. (The stationary part can be called a "stator," but is usually designated the "field" section.) Once in the rotor, this energy appears as an alternating current. As such, it sets up an alternating magnetic field around the rotor. This field interacts with the field present in the "field" part of the motor, much as our loop's field interacts with the field between the poles of the magnet. And so the rotor spins.

Current is not fed through wires and brushes to the rotor of such a motor but is *induced* by means of the constantly reversing field of the stationary part of the motor. This kind of motor is called an *induction* motor.

Although an electric car will carry batteries that produce DC, they may well use AC motors. Direct current from a battery can be converted easily to AC, but at some cost. A design engineer may decide to accept this cost if he or she finds advantages to AC operations that outweigh it. Besides, even DC electric-car motors may be of a special type that has some features of AC operation. What's more, the energy source for an electric car may not be simply a battery. It may not be a battery at all. It has already been mentioned that an electric-car motor may be "universal," running on either type of power.

Not only will induction motors not run on DC; they will not run at all unless they are running. This sounds like a strange statement, but all it means is that an induction motor is not self-starting. Once it is started, however, and gets up to speed, it operates very efficiently.

Most AC motors, including all that are stronger than mousepower, are induction motors. That may seem strange, since we have just said that induction motors are not self-starting. Though there are some very old electric clocks that have to be started by hand, every AC motor one is likely to run across starts spinning the moment the switch is thrown. What's the catch?

The catch is that most induction motors do not operate as induction motors until they have come up to speed. They even have brushes. When the motor is first turned on, the brushes feed current to the rotor, and it begins to spin. At this time, all

The Islander is a prototype vehicle from Transportation Systems Laboratory of New Bedford, Massachusetts. It was made as a convertible, as shown, and as a station-wagon body. Various batteries for different ranges of speed and cruising range are available. (*Transportation Systems*)

the coils, etc., inside the motor are connected like an old-fashioned, noninduction motor. But when the right speed is reached, a "speed-sensitive" switch throws, and reconnects everything to make up an induction motor. This switch is located right on the shaft of the motor, inside the motor housing.

Speed-sensitive motor switches are very important. They are included in many motors that are not induction motors, including DC motors. They will be essential in motors that power electric cars. The "why" of a speed-sensitive switch is important. Not how it works, though that might be interesting. Why does any motor need one? A brief reconsideration of gasoline engines will help to answer the question.

A gasoline engine is never started under load. When a standard shift car is being started, the transmission is in neutral. At least, the driver has his foot on the clutch pedal, so that the transmission (gears) and the wheels are not connected to the engine. Once the engine is started, and gets up to some kind of speed, the operator moves the shift lever to *first gear*. This arranges the gears in the transmission so that the "mechanical advantage" is with the engine. It can turn fast, to make the wheels turn slowly. Then the driver lets out the clutch—that is, he lets up smoothly on the pedal. Gradually, this connects the engine to the transmission and wheels. The car slowly begins to move. The engine, again, is turning fast, but the wheels are turning slowly. Gradually the car picks up speed. When it has enough speed, the driver shifts to a different gear ratio. This allows the engine to run a little more slowly for a given speed. Finally, in high gear, with the car up to cruising speed, the engine isn't working as hard as it was at the beginning. It is making relatively few turns per second, compared to the many turns the wheels are making on the road.

With an automatic-transmission car, the same things are happening, even though the driver has no clutch pedal and just pops a "shift" lever to the *drive* position. He or she still starts the engine with that lever in the *neutral* or *park* position. The engine starts, idles, comes up to speed, develops some torque. Once it has torque and the driver shifts to *drive*, clutching and gear-shifting still go on. They are automatic, but they happen.

It is very difficult to get an engine started, and get it to stay "started" and to run, and to develop any power to speak of, if the engine has a "load" on it. The load is the weight and inertia of the car. (Inertia is defined by the phrase, "a body at rest tends to remain at rest unless acted upon by a force.") The car is the body at rest, and a heavy one at that. The engine is going to supply that moving force. But first it must get up some force. It develops the force as torque, and to have lots of torque, the engine must turn rapidly.

There is another thing. It takes more energy to accelerate a body than to keep it moving at constant speed. More gasoline is burned in every second when a car is accelerating than in any second when running at constant speed, in any gear. Gasoline burned means energy expended. What we call "power" is amount-of-energy-per-unit-of-time, so it takes more power to accelerate a car—that is, change its speed—than to keep it rolling.

Suppose the car were electric. The same thing is true. More electricity must be used to get the car rolling and accelerate it up to cruising speed than to keep it there.

Now, one advantage to an electric motor is that it can start under load. It may start poorly and slowly, depending on design, or it may start very well. However, induction motors, which, as was said before, "will not run unless they are running," are an exception. Given a proper design, a brush-type electric motor can start very well under load. Even under a heavy load. But the heavier the load, the more current the motor will demand during start-up.

A motor designed to start well under load may not run well or may run efficiently only at high speeds. It will probably draw too much current at any speed. Other designs draw less current for a given amount of torque or a given rotor speed, but they are not as peppy at starting under load. Although most induction motors can be started with a hand-spin of the shaft if no load is connected, it would be difficult to get an induction motor up to its operating speed by hand cranking if it is under load.

Most motors have speed-sensitive switches. Depending on

the position of the switch, the motor windings are connected to make up one kind of a motor or another. Practically any motor is designed to operate this way. A DC motor may start as a high-current, low-speed, low-efficiency type and then switch to low-current, high-speed, high-efficiency operation at the right intermediate speed. An induction motor can start as a high-current, low-speed brush type and then switch itself to efficient, fast induction operation at the right speed. In theory, at least, an induction motor could start as a DC motor and become an AC motor when its speed was right.

The mechanical versatility of electric motors gives the design engineer many options. He might think that he would like to get rid of the clutch. In most electric motor applications, clutches are not used. Why should they be used in electric cars? So he wants high torque under load for the motor's starting condition. But that demands a lot of current. Even if his electric car is on a trolley, taking current from city mains, that puts quite a load on the system. It is also inefficient. So he can design his motor to switch to a different mode of operation, drawing less current once it has some speed. If the car's power supply is a set of batteries, this arrangement saves battery drain. In fact, using a simple converter to change battery DC into AC, the engineer may be able to get his motor to operate as an AC motor. This has a number of advantages.

The designer may wish his motor to operate like an AC motor even if it is a DC motor being fed from batteries. That is, he might not want to use *steady* current, even though it is there. (A direct current flows steadily, like water in a small, constant-pressure pipe.) He might want to feed the current in *pulses*—not true alternating pulses, as in AC, but just turning the current on and off at a rapid rate. Why? Because pulse operation can give some options in both speed and power control.

Suppose a DC motor system has power supplied to it in a succession of rather short pulses. Assume that twenty pulses are

The Witkar (Dutch for "white car") has been a commercial success in Amsterdam. The Witkar is rented on an as-needed basis to members of an association. The cars are parked at stations located at various points throughout the city. Each member has a key. To use a Witkar, the key-holder inserts the key into a control box on the steering column. The driver dials a code for his destination, another Witkar station. A central computer then charges the driver according to the miles driven. Batteries are recharged at the stations. The Witkar has a top speed of about 18 miles per hour. (*Xerox Education Publications. Photo by G. Bedding*)

sent in every second. Assume further that each pulse is ¼₀ of a second long, so that there is a ¼₀-second rest between pulses. If designed properly, the motor would spin. Its rotor would receive a little shove from each pulse and coast a bit between pulses.

There are more things that can be done to the pulses. They could be made shorter, with longer rests, or with more pulses per second. Depending on the ratio of pulses to rests, more or less power could be delivered to speed the motor up or slow it down. The strength of the pulses—that is, the voltage—could be raised or lowered. For a given electrical resistance in the load, the current being drawn is proportional to the voltage. (Remember, voltage can be thought of as if it were pressure, as in a water hose, and current can be thought of as "amount," again as in a water system.) Power, in electric circuits, always equals current-times-voltage, and it is expressed in watts.

The trains of pulses could be timed to deliver quite a bit of power to the motor but to make it run slowly. That is, you could have "high" pulses, but space them out. "Low" pulses (but lots of them) could be delivered to let the motor run along at a high, smooth speed. This might save battery current.

Conceivably, a pulsed-DC motor might even be made to operate like an AC induction motor. This eliminates brushes and commutator. Brushes and commutators both wear, because there is sliding friction. Also, there can be heavy loss of energy through the brush-and-commutator contact. Usually there is *arcing* (sparking) where brushes and commutator meet, causing both power losses and erosion of the parts. Arcing also causes "static" interference in radios, TV sets, even computers, control systems, and telephone systems. The radio or computer or whatever need not be installed in the car to suffer from this interference. It need only be nearby.

So, there is every reason for the designer to get rid of brushes, commutators, and other contact points when possible. At least, he hopes not to use them once the motor and the car are up to speed. He may still need them just to get the motor under load.

A pulsed motor *may* be equivalent to an induction motor because turning a direct current rapidly on and off makes it, in effect, like an alternating current. At the start of each pulse, a magnetic field expands out from the conductor carrying the current. When the pulse is turned off, the field collapses (it does not simply "disappear"). Either way, this magnetic field is a *moving* field. Now, it happens that a magnetic field moving past a conductor will induce an electric current in that conductor.

The "how" of this current induction involves some detailed physics. But there is one thing about almost everything that happens in physics. That is, almost everything "runs both ways." For example, we have just noted that a magnetic field moving past a conductor will make an electric current flow in that conductor, and earlier we saw that a current moving through a conductor will generate a magnetic field around the conductor. (That is how the loop motor worked.)

There is more—still another way this physics works: Moving a conductor inside a magnetic field will also make a current flow in the conductor. This is because it doesn't matter whether the field moves or the conductor moves. From the point of view of either of them, the *other* is moving. (This is part of the principle of relativity.)

Producing electricity by moving a conductor inside a magnetic field is called electromagnetic induction. The principle of electromagnetic induction makes the induction motor possible. That is, because of this queer property of matter and energy, it is possible to get electric energy into the spinning rotor of a motor without connecting any wires or brushes to it. By extension, this same thing makes a pulsed-DC "induction-type" motor possible.

Another practical application of electromagnetic induction

is that an electric motor can be turned around to make it a generator. Instead of putting electricity in so that the shaft will turn and do some work, the shaft can be turned by some means and electricity will be produced. This is no mere curiosity. Right now, any generator that makes electricity is really a motor. There are minor design differences, just as there are design differences between motors built for different tasks. *But most motors can be used as generators.*

The dual nature of electric motors is significant for electric cars. First, generators recharge batteries. Second, making the car move by any means makes the generator spin and produce electricity.

The movement of the car may provide some "free" recharging of the batteries of an electric car, but not all the time. Not when the motor is being a motor, and is drawing current from the battery. However, while running downhill, the car can be propelled by gravity with a small assist from the car's inertia. That is, the car was moving before it even started downhill. There is quite a bit of energy stored in its motion. The motor could just as well be switched off. Suppose, while the car is going downhill, the axle is left connected to the motor shaft so that the wheels turn the motor? Now the motor is a generator. Electricity is coming out of it.

In principle at least, this electricity can be put back into the battery, provided, of course, that the battery is of the secondary or "storage" type. The concept is not new. In the 1920s many cars were equipped with starter motors that served as generators when the car was moving. Putting the electricity into the battery means hooking it back up to the motor. Won't the motor then simply act like a motor, draw current from the battery, and speed the downhill run of the car? No, for the simple reason that a motor and a generator are each connected to a battery in a different way. The control system will take care of that.

There are some problems. The generator must be turning at the correct rate, generating the proper voltage, and this will take some automatic adjustment. But the techniques, and even the parts, for that adjustment have already been worked out for the generators on gasoline cars.

Using the motor as a generator gives another dividend: braking. Just as a motor can be spun freely by hand if no load is connected to it, so can a generator. But if a load is connected to either, it becomes hard to turn. For a generator, such a load is the battery being charged. The more current the generator is delivering, the harder it is to turn. This means that an electric car cannot coast freely if its motor has been switched around for use as a generator. The motor-battery combination then acts as a drag on the wheels; it tends to slow the car down, a desirable circumstance when going downhill.

Suppose, for various reasons, the motor-generator happens to be switched out of the battery circuit. This happens with a gasoline car's generator whenever the battery has all the charge it can take at the moment. For braking purposes, the motor-generator can be switched to a *resistive load*. This will just be some poor conductor of electricity that tends to heat up when current flows through it. The mechanical motion of the car's wheels will then be converted to heat in the resistor, and the car will slow down.

Switching an electric car's motor to the generator mode, and to either the battery or the resistive load for braking, can be automatic. The way most designers envision the control systems of electric cars, the car will go into braking automatically the moment the driver takes his foot off the accelerator.

An electric car would still have friction brakes. At least it would have some kind of definite brake on each wheel in addition to the motor–battery–resistive load system of electric braking. Electric braking is not very strong at very *low* speeds. In a way this is an advantage—braking is regulated by the amount

The Electric Free Propulsion Corporation has produced a number of electric cars. Some are built completely as electrics and others are based on existing gasoline-car bodies. The company, in cooperation with Holiday Inns, has installed charging stations at Holiday Inns along Interstate 94 between Detroit and Chicago.

The X-144, introduced in 1973, is based on the AMC Gremlin. It is equipped with a lead-cobalt battery. A compound of cobalt, dissolved in the sulfuric acid electrolyte, forms a coating on the positive grid. This coating greatly reduces the formation of various harmful gases during recharging. The X-144 is also equipped with a 12-volt accessory battery for lights, horn, heaters, and blowers. Maximum speed is about 60 miles per hour. Range is fifty to a hundred miles, depending on speed.

The Mars II and the EFP Battery Van. The Mars II, based on the Renault 10, is also equipped with lead-cobalt batteries (four 30-volt, 290-amp-hour batteries). Theoretically, lead-cobalt batteries can deliver about twice as much energy per pound as ordinary lead-acid. The Mars II has a range of about 120 miles at 30 miles per hour, and about sixty miles at 60 miles per hour. Power is delivered through a four-speed manual transmission. The van has no transmission, running on direct drive from the motor. Reversing is accomplished through a switch. (*General Electric Company*)

of braking needed. But at some point a foot brake that the driver presses would come into play.

Compared to gasoline engines, electric motors lack good horsepower-to-weight ratios. A 200-horsepower electric motor is much bigger and heavier than a 200-horsepower V-8 engine. However, electric cars would not need such horsepower ratings. For most purposes—such as in-town shopping—they would be going rather slowly, perhaps no more than 25 miles an hour. (This is as good an average speed as a gasoline car can hope to make in city traffic anyway.) Not only that; electric motors are much more efficient than gasoline engines. The best efficiency attainable for a gasoline engine is around 30 to 35 per cent. That is, 30 to 35 per cent of the energy in the fuel actually goes into the turning of the engine. The rest is wasted as heat. However, even this efficiency is that of the engine alone. Hook up a transmission, clutch, the entire "power train" out to the wheels, figure in wheel-bearing friction and tire-flexing losses and tire-road slippage, and efficiency may be 7 to 10 per cent.

An electric motor can be as efficient as 90 to 95 per cent. Even given imperfect design, most motors are at least 85 per cent efficient. Since the power train can be simpler in an electric car, much less energy is lost getting traction power to the wheels than in gasoline cars. Even assuming the worst losses in a complicated car design, the motor will work out to be three to five times as efficient as a gasoline engine, driving a car of the same weight at the same speeds. Another way of saying this is that one horsepower delivered by an electric motor is the equivalent of 3 to 5 horsepower in a gasoline engine.

For stationary electric motors, design engineers usually have not had to worry much about size and weight, or horsepower-to-pound ratio, except perhaps in order to be thrifty with materials. For mobile use, an electric motor needs to be comparatively small and light, with a good horsepower-to-weight ratio. The weight of batteries or other energy sources is considerable. The motor should not have to waste power "just pulling itself around."

However, the electric-motor design engineer also has quite a bag of tricks. As has been noted, he can even make a motor be several types at once, switching from one type to another depending on the kind of operation required or desired at the moment. With the instant flick of a switch—and an automatic switch at that—the motor can be converted into a generator and perhaps "give back" some of the energy of the motion of the car. The motor can be used as brake, too. This does not mean that the options are unlimited, or that all of them can be used at once, or that all the combinations of options are within reasonable cost.

For example, a motor that is going to demand very heavy currents under starting loads will need very heavy wire in its "loop" or coil windings. But to take advantage of the strength of magnetic field built into the motor, many turns of wire are needed in a small space. Also, there are advantages to operating a motor at fairly high voltages, and that requires many turns of wire. But many turns of heavy wire will mean that certain parts of the motor must be bigger, bulkier, and heavier; and size, weight, and expense are three things a designer wants to keep to a minimum.

All engineering design is a matter of trade-offs. Suppose you had to design a rather small cargo-carrying airplane for small airports with short runways. Should it be designed for maximum weight capacity, maximum cruising range, and minimum takeoff and landing distances? What kind of speed should it have? Also, what about fuel economy? If it is designed in favor of the other factors it may need a big, thirsty engine. A successful design will be a good compromise between all these conflicting specifications. It is quite possible to design a plane that will perform like a champion in *most* of the specifications, but it might be so expensive that no airline would buy it.

Electric propulsion is also helping to take the noise and fumes out of weekends in suburbia. The E12M Elec-Trak, one of a line of electric tractors, is manufactured by General Electric. This lawn tractor is equipped with a 42-inch mower. It has three forward speeds and two reverse in three gear ranges for a total of nine forward speeds. (*General Electric Company*)

The electric-car designer has similar problems. He must figure the trade-offs correctly. He must be able to keep the price down by designing for ease of manufacture and economy of materials. He must consider safety and durability. The car needs reasonable speed, but it also must be efficient. What kind of energy source should be used? And will the kind that looks best from the standpoint of price, or reliability, or convenience, or all three, really be right for the "best" motor and control system he can come up with?

Actually, there are several different sets of designers looking for these trade-offs. Good motor designers are not usually good battery or fuel-cell designers, and vise versa. Neither are they likely to be top-notch body and power-train designers. Each set of specialists has to leave some aspects of car design to the other sets of specialists.

4

CONTROLS

Any car has controls. We need hardly name them for a gasoline car. Everyone is conscious of steering wheel, accelerator pedal, brake pedal, gearshift lever, perhaps clutch pedal, and, of course, the ignition key. Turn-signal and headlight controls are essential even in "stripped down" cars. Then there are controls for the windshield wiper. Finally, there are accessory controls— for heater or air conditioning, for a radio, for power-operated windows. Luxury cars may have more controls still—that is, visible controls.

Present-day and future electric cars are likely to have fewer and less complicated hand- and foot-operated controls than their early-part-of-the-century ancestors. The following is from the 1915 Rauch and Lang "Selective Dual Control" model owner's manual.

To Operate Electric

(1) *Be seated.*

(2) *Place steering lever in position to give ready control.*

(3) *Insert key in controller handle and unlock.*

(4) *Pull controller handle back to brake or off position and raise slide. (This closes the circuit and electric is ready to move.)*

(5) *Be sure that the foot brake is released.*

(6) *Forward movement of the controller handle gives two starting speeds and three running speeds.*

(7) *To stop electric, pull controller handle backward past off position. First the electric brake will come into action and then a mechanical motor brake.*

(8) *To reverse, bring electric to standstill. Press down the foot lever. Move controller handle forward same as when running forward. Two starting and one running speed will be obtained when backing up.*

(9) *To stop reversing, pull controller handle to extreme backward position. Take foot off reverse lever, which will automatically return to forward position and electric is ready to be operated in a forward direction.*

(10) *Steering: Push steering arm from you to turn to the left and pull steering arm toward you to turn to the right.*

(11) *When leaving the electric, be sure to always force down slide of controller handle and take key out of lock.*

(12) *Release foot brake before applying power.*

The best-known electric car in the world and out of it is the Lunar Rover. Here Astronaut David Scott is on the Rover waiting for Astronaut James Irwin to get aboard after an Apollo 15 rock-gathering session. Weighing about 480 pounds, the Rover is powered by two silver-zinc batteries. There is a motor in each of the four wheels. The wheels, made of flexible wire mesh, can turn independently. A built-in navigation system tells the astronauts at all times the direction and distance back to the lunar module. (*NASA*)

A gasoline car has a few invisible controls. There is one set, under the hood, that regulates the voltage and current coming from the car's electric generator. The voltage is regulated to keep the *charge rate* to the battery constant at different engine speeds. The carburetor has some automatic controls to regulate the mixing of air and gasoline vapor going into the cylinders (automatic choke). The starter has an automatic device that disconnects the starter's machinery from the engine once the engine starts running by itself. There are, in some cars, various electronic ignition controls. And there are many more, automatic and out of sight.

An electric car needs controls for steering and braking, of course, and it also needs the equivalent of an accelerator. While electric cars are "simpler" in many ways than gasoline cars, they still need many controls, most of them automatic. Mainly they need *switching* and *regulating* controls, more so than a gasoline car does.

As one might expect, electric cars need more electrical controls than gasoline cars. People are accustomed to having many accessories, even luxuries, in cars today. Electric cars are likely to have radios, heaters, windshield wipers and washers, even air conditioning. Some people may demand power windows. There are headlights, taillights, turn signals, dome lights, and instrument lights. And of course there are one or more electric motors for propulsion, possibly electric braking, and possibly more than one bank of batteries.

In gasoline cars, electric switches and controls involve low voltages and (except for the starter and generator) small currents. In an electric car, much higher voltages and heavier currents have to be switched.

At first glance, all this seems to be a simple matter. Switches are an old invention. So are "intensity" controls, like the volume control on a radio, or the speed control on an electric mixer.

Remember, however, that many of the switches and intensity controls on an electric car have to be automatic. A switch or a control for a low voltage and a small current is one design problem, but switches and controls for high voltages and heavy currents are quite another.

Heavy currents mean *big* switches, heavy ones. Ordinary switches have *contact points* and resistance at those points has to be kept low. Also, high voltages mean arcing, and arcing eats metal, wastes power, and interferes with true abrupt on-off control.

Also, familiar controls like volume controls work by increasing the circuit resistance, and *consuming some of the power*. In a radio or stereo, the volume controls are in a very low-power part of the circuit, ahead of the main amplifier stages. The amount of power "wasted" and the amount of heat produced is negligible. Simple resistance controls will not be the answer for electric automobiles, however. Heavy current has to pass through these controls.

Not only do electric-automobile controls have to be automatic, but many will have to operate simultaneously. Sets of controls sometimes have to operate in patterns of on-off, high-low. For safety and other reasons, electric cars may have to switch in electric braking the moment the driver takes his foot off the speed pedal. This involves switching connections between drive motors and batteries, and switching coils within the motors, all without any driver decisions.

So, the control system for an electric car will have to carry some "logic" circuits, something like those in a computer. The automatic switches are electrically controlled. A switch that is itself thrown by electricity is called a *relay*. But relays, especially heavy ones for heavy currents, can demand large amounts of electricity themselves.

Engineers have been developing switches and control systems for more than a hundred years. But the electric car will probably demand something new. Not something brand new or something not even dreamed of yet, but some new developments. Some of these developments are in the "solid-state" field, the same field of science that produced the transistor in the 1950s.

At its simplest, a switch is simply two pieces of metal that can be made to touch or not touch. When they are touching,

The copper Electric Van III is a prototype made by the Copper Development Association. Batteries, motor, and transmission are all situated in front to allow maximum load and space in the rear. (*Copper Development Association*)

electricity can flow from one to the other. If they are not touching, electricity cannot flow.

A switch is a convenience. If a dry cell is hooked up to a light bulb, the only way to turn the lamp off is to disconnect one of the wires. (There is no need to disconnect both. No electricity can flow unless there is a complete circuit.) So, if we insert a movable piece of metal into the circuit we can make and break the circuit easily. This simple switch, as reliable as it is, has several limitations. The most obvious is that someone has to be there to operate it. In addition, it can operate only as fast and as accurately as the human running it.

A relay is operated by an electromagnet. The contacts of the relay are made of iron. No one has to be anywhere near it to make it operate. In fact, relays on spacecraft millions of miles away are operated by radio. Relays operate very fast, and if two or more are hooked into a circuit, they will all operate at exactly the same time.

Relays were invented for telegraph service. For long telegraph lines, signals would get weak, because of resistance, after a hundred miles or so. The use of more, stronger batteries at the sending and receiving points did not help a great deal. It just meant more waste. Of course, at each station along a route, an operator could receive and copy a message and then send it to the next station. But this was slow. However, suppose a relay switch replaced the telegraph receiver? The relay switch could use the weak signal from the lines to operate fresh *local* batteries that both operated a local sounder and sent a new strong signal to the next station at the same time. For long lines crossing the prairies or the mountains, going hundreds of miles between towns, unmanned relay stations could keep the signals moving.

Since a relay can be operated by another relay, the relay switch soon found uses in control systems, both for automatic operation and for human safety.

In a gasoline car, when the starter switch is turned, the circuit of a relay coil is closed. This operation takes only a small amount of electricity. The ignition switch is small and the wires between it, the battery, and the relay are of small diameter. This arrangement is economical, both of wire and electricity. The relay contact arm closes a circuit between the battery and the starter. This circuit has short and heavy wires, because a very heavy current is used in the starter.

Also, in any car, the high-low headlight beam system uses a relay. It is a relay under the hood that sends battery current into either the high beam or the low beam headlamp, not the simple switch under your left foot.

Electric cars also need voltage and current controls, similar to a volume control. The simplest types have a moving "switch" contact that "wipes" against a long contact made of a material that does not conduct electricity very well. Such a material will have a high amount of resistance per unit of length. When the wiper arm is near the end of this contact that is connected to the circuit, not much of the material is between the wiper arm and the rest of the circuit, so resistance is fairly low. When the wiper arm is moved farther away, more of the resistive material is in the circuit, and resistance is high.

When resistance is high, electrical energy is being used up, turned into heat. The control itself gets warmer. For high-voltage, heavy-current, high-power applications, this is not only wasteful; it could be dangerous.

For alternating current, there are various ways of controlling currents and voltages that use the *induction* effect and do not waste too much power or generate too much heat. But for direct current, the induction effect cannot be used. To get around this difficulty, some heavy-duty DC circuits were controlled for many years by use of vacuum tubes. In recent years, solid-state or transistor-type devices have been under development. In either a vacuum tube or a transistor, *a small electric current can be used to control a large one.* As the small current varies, so the large one can be made to vary, *in step.*

For example, in a vacuum-tube circuit, changes of a few hundredths or even thousandths of a volt in the control side of the circuit can cause changes of several volts, or several tens of volts, in the "load" part of the circuit. These large changes in voltage result in changes in the amount of current drawn and in the amount of power delivered. In a high-fidelity or electric-guitar amplifier, the weak fluctuating music signal from the record, tape, or guitar is amplified in this way: changes in this weak signal cause identical changes in a much stronger flow of electricity at the speaker end of the circuit.

Transistors rather than vacuum tubes are used in most electronic devices today. *How* a transistor or a tube works is beyond the scope of this book. Basically, the controlling of a strong electric flow by means of a weak one is what they do.

Engineers are developing transistorlike devices that are "gates" or "valves" for the heavy currents and high voltages that will power the drive motors of electric cars. There are some problems. One is that transistors are not as sensitive as vacuum tubes are. That is, the control current cannot be microscopic as compared to the current being controlled. Then why not use vacuum tubes? For many reasons. One of the main ones is that vacuum tubes have a *filament*, like a light bulb's, that has to be heated up to a certain temperature before the tube will work. This consumes a great deal of electric power and generates much heat.

Another problem with solid-state control is that the best, most promising devices have to be made of silicon, or other "tricky" materials. Silicon is a common element—all glass contains it, and so do all granite rocks (the most common rocks found on land). Quartz crystals are just silicon and oxygen, or silicon dioxide. But transistor silicon has to be refined to a high degree of purity. This is an expensive process. Then, to make the transistor, the silicon has to be carefully "doped" with traces of other elements. This is again a difficult, expensive process—the bigger the transistor, the more difficult and expensive. The same thing goes for the other main kind of solid-state device, the silicon diode. The bigger it is and the more current it has to handle, the more difficult it is to make. And the less reliable.

Also, solid-state devices do not take well to high voltages. The easiest way to get high power in a circuit is to use a relatively high voltage with a fairly small current. It is possible to get high power the other way around, but that requires heavier wires, heavier everything (and, for battery circuits, more battery cells).

Still, progress in solid-state development has been rapid. Only a few years ago, people scoffed at the idea of the solid-state *chip* circuit, in which dozens or hundreds of tiny transistors and diodes are built upon a silicon "chip" hardly bigger than a pinhead. The complicated electronic systems of the Project Apollo moon-flight spaceships were made possible by this development. Today's compact electronic computers use hundreds, or even thousands, of these chips. As electric cars become more sophisticated, they are more likely to use chips as well.

The silicon chip was called an "industrial miracle." It is not a miracle, but it is superb engineering. Engineering of the same quality is being applied to the problem of *big* solid-state devices for electric cars.

The control system for an electric car might include a few large old-fashioned relays and many solid-state or silicon devices. The complete system will switch battery connections to provide. highest voltage when needed (batteries in series) or high current when needed (batteries in parallel). At the same time, the system will switch windings in the drive motors to take whatever voltage-current combination is needed for hill-climbing, ac-

Detroit auto manfacturers are also engaged in electric car research. Shown here are some of the experimental electric vehicles from the Ford Motor Company. Above, the Berliner is equipped with lead-acid batteries. Below, the Comita (left) was designed from the start as an electric car, while the E-car (right) is based on the Ford Cortina. The E-car has both nickel-cadmium and lead-acid batteries. It was designed as an experiment to determine whether a station-wagon-sized electric car could keep up with modern traffic. The company also did research into the feasibility of using sodium-sulfur cells. (*Ford Motor Company*)

celerating, cruising at low speed, or cruising at high speed. When the driver takes his foot off the accelerator pedal, the system will probably switch the motors into a resistance braking mode.

A solid-state control system may be able to accomplish something else. It may be able to convert the steady direct current of the battery supply into a *pulsating* current for feeding the motors. By varying the "height" of the pulses (their voltage) or the length of the pulses (the time taken up by each pulse), the system will feed more or less current to the drive motors. Not only that, but such a system should vary pulse voltage and length automatically.

That is where "logic" circuits and the small chips come in. The logic circuitry will function something like a computer. It will be measuring—*all the time*—the amount of current being used, the voltage available, the speed of the car, and the driver's "demand" (that is, whether his foot is heavy or light on the accelerator pedal). Depending on all these factors, it will vary the amount of power being fed the drive motor, for cruising, hill-climbing, and so forth.

All the basics of solid-state control are known. So are all the basics of making various solid-state devices. No real breakthroughs are needed. It is a task of *development*, which is another way of saying time and money.

5

THE FUTURE OF
THE ELECTRIC CAR

There can be little doubt that electric cars, of one kind or another, will become a greater part of the transportation scene in
the years ahead. The world's supply of petroleum is not infinite.
Indeed, it is quite limited. Over the long view, the "petroleum
age" may turn out to be one of the shortest "ages" in history.
It is no small irony that one of the shortest ages in human history will have taken one of the longest periods of geological history for its preparation. Hundreds of millions of years were

required for the remains of dead plants and animals to be converted to petroleum. History may indeed record that humankind used it all up in less than two hundred years.

Although it may seem logical to assume that people will start using electric cars when there is no more gasoline to run internal-combustion engines, there is an important hitch to this assumption. The hitch is that most electricity is made by burning petroleum. If all the cars running around in the mid-1970s were suddenly to become electric cars, there would not be enough electricity to run them all. If petroleum-burning power plants started to produce electricity to run them, the result could be a dangerous increase in air pollution, a situation that would seem to defeat the idea that electric cars are supposed to reduce air pollution.

Without an adequate supply of electricity to charge batteries or run electric cars directly, such cars can be little more than curiosities. So it would seem that the key to the success of electric cars is an ample, nonpolluting source of electricity. And that supply of electricity has to become less and less dependent on petroleum.

Nuclear energy has been proposed as one way to produce electricity with less dependence on fossil fuels. Many scientists believe that nuclear plants are dangerous. Harmful radiation can "leak" from the plants during their operation. An accident could possibly result in a "melt-down" that could release large amounts of radiation into the air. Then there is the problem of what to do with the waste materials. The wastes are very dangerous radioactive materials. They stay dangerous for thousands of years. There is no completely safe way of storing nuclear-power-plant waste products.

Many other ways of producing electricity have been proposed. After the oil boycott of 1974, much more attention was given to the possibility of using the power of the sun directly. Solar heat could be used to make steam to drive generators.

Electricity could also be obtained directly from the sun through the use of solar cells. Solar cells are thin metal disks in which an electric current is induced when they are exposed to light.

One of the most far-reaching proposals is the building of a rather special kind of electric generator out in the oceans. This generator would work on the energy of the differences in temperature between the surface and the deeper layers of water. The electricity would then be brought to land via cables.

Then there are windmills. One might not think of wind power as solar power. But without the sun there would be no heating of the atmosphere and therefore no wind. Windmills can be hooked up to electric generators. By the mid-1970s, windmill generators for home use were widely available.

All of these so-called alternative sources are likely to be more important in the overall economy by the turn of the century. As oil becomes more scarce, more time and money will be expended on alternate energy sources.

It is possible that solar and wind energy might be used directly for electric cars. The cars could be equipped with banks of solar cells on the roof. Of course, these would work only in the daytime and on sunny days at that. But while they were working, the solar cells would be feeding current into the batteries. This arrangement would seem to be almost a free ride. The ride would not be quite free. The solar cells are very expensive. But various lines of research in the 1970s had the promise of bringing the price down. From time to time, solar-cell-equipped electric cars are displayed in automobile shows, as curiosities.

Some of the Witkar stations in Amsterdam (see page 63) have windmill generators for recharging batteries. This concept could be extended to charging stations that would operate much as gas stations do today.

Mounting a windmill-driven generator on the roof of an electric car is an intriguing possibility, if only for its novelty. A

windmill on the roof implies a sort of perpetual-motion machine that would be powered by the motion of the car itself.
That is, the wind resulting from the motion of the car would
turn the windmill generator, which in turn would charge the
battery to move the car some more. Of course it wouldn't work,
not as a free ride anyway. The windmill might provide some
recharge current while the car is parked. And it could also provide usable current on downhill runs. But, as mentioned earlier,
the wheels could do that. However, despite its limitations, some
manufacturers just might offer cars with windmill generators if
doing so would not add too much to the price and weight of
the car.

Price is, of course, an important factor in the success of
electric cars. Equally as important are operating costs. After the
1974 Arab oil boycott, the price of electricity in most parts of
the United States and Canada started to go up, and it appeared
that it would continue to rise. *Consumer Reports* maintained
that a high-mileage gasoline car such as the Honda was more
economical to run than two electric cars that were reviewed in
the same issue, especially in high-electricity-cost areas such as
the Northeast.

The heavier city traffic is, the more successful electric cars
are likely to be. Stop-and-go city driving is the most expensive
way to use a gasoline car. A lot of fuel is wasted in engine
idling. The stop and go is also hard on the car, particularly the
engine. Brakes, transmission, and other parts are also excessively
worn in city driving. The spark plugs can get fouled and the
engine can overheat.

Electric cars overcome the wastefulness of city driving
through one small but significant mechanical fact. That is,
when an electric car stops, the motor stops. There is no current
drain while the driver of an electric car waits for the traffic light
to change. If a gasoline engine were shut off and started each

time the car had to be stopped and started in traffic, engine life would be severely cut and the battery quickly used up.

On the open highway, the advantage belongs to the gasoline car. Steady driving at reasonable speeds (40–60 miles per hour) brings out the greatest economy in operating a gasoline car. The same speeds would quickly drain the batteries of an electric car. Eventually, electric-car technology might be advanced to the point where electric cars could run at highway speeds long enough between changes to make the trip worthwhile. However, such a car would be very expensive with the batteries and power packs available in the 1970s. Yet polls have shown that some sort of market for electric cars exists right now. Many people would welcome them for short-distance, low-speed city runs. The electric car has a great deal going for it. Costs can be brought down, not only by technical improvements but by the ways in which batteries, cars, or both are marketed and used.

Besides, people are very pollution-conscious these days. More and more people—young people, especially—take well to the idea of transportation without poisonous fumes and without too much noise. An electric car makes very little noise as it rolls along, and when it is stopped, it makes none. Not just when it is parked or turned off but also when it is pausing at a traffic light, the car is silent. As mentioned before, all the moving parts on an all-electric car stop when the car stops.

Responding to this, the automobile industry may decide to promote electric cars, at least as a "second car" backup to the gasoline car. Until very recently, Detroit tended to put most of its energy into preserving the internal-combustion engine as America's main power source. Development effort has gone into catalytic converters (to burn up unused gasoline and carbon monoxide) and other antismog devices for the gasoline engine.

In the mid-1960s, Detroit's attitude was that legal smog

and pollution standards really couldn't be met. By 1971, Detroit was predicting that it could surpass legal standards. But well before that time, all the major motor companies were building, or somehow had a hand in, experimental electric vehicles.

There is no way now of predicting whether the internal-combustion piston engine can be "rescued" as the number-one power source. It has competition. Gas turbines, which resemble the engines of a typical turbojet airliner, are a contender, as are Wankel engines. Steam cars, which did fairly well in the early 1900s, are another. So are cousins to the steam car which use freon or other vapors in place of true steam. However, concern over fluorocarbons in the atmosphere (freon is a fluorocarbon) may have killed that idea. In the far future, one of these might possibly emerge as the true rival of the gasoline engine as *the* power source for large, fast, long-distance automobiles.

However, the electric motor has a long head start. For getting rid of pollution, it offers the best promise. As polls have shown, the quiet, smog-free electric car already has a niche waiting for it. Progress with better batteries and fuel cells has been rapid in recent years. The space program spurred development at first, but now the demand for a smog-free "in-town" car has brought more companies and more talent into the search for a better battery.

Everyone is aware that the population of the United States will probably pass 300 million by the year 2000, from the 1970 count of 210 million or so. Even with improved public transportation, the demand for automobiles is sure to keep rising along with population. So will the demand for roads. And so will pollution from internal-combustion engines, unless substitute power sources are developed.

People want clean, healthful air to breathe. People are tired of congestion on the streets and highways. One reason for the large sale of foreign and domestic compact cars is that they are small, they are easier to maneuver and park, and they take up less room on the road. Even with something of a cost penalty, an electric with good in-town performance could be welcome on the market.

Future electric cars could be available in many varieties. They will range in type from very small all-electric golf-cart types to hybrid cars, which use both electric motors and some kind of engine.

Hybrid cars are not new. The Woods Motor Vehicle Company, maker of Woods electrics from 1899 to 1919, produced something called the "Dual Power" in 1917. In addition to an electric motor, the car had a four-cylinder 12-horsepower gasoline engine. The engine could be used to charge the batteries or run the car.

In the late 1960s, General Motors experimented with a hybrid electric fitted with a Stirling engine, batteries, and an electric motor. The Stirling engine is an external-combustion engine. A working fluid, hydrogen gas, expands on heating and pushes a power piston, the lower of two pistons, in a single cylinder. An upper piston opens and closes ports in the cylinder walls. The energy for heating the hydrogen comes from burning kerosene. The Stirling engine has a much cleaner exhaust than gasoline engines. The engine in the GM car was used only to charge the batteries, not to move the car directly.

"Golf-cart" types of electric vehicles might be used as "motorized supermarket baskets." One of these might be picked up in the parking lot of a carless shopping district. The parking lot could also be a public-transportation station. The parking-lot or public-transportation fee would include the use of the battery carts. The cart is loaded with purchases as it is driven from store to store. The little car will probably run on special lanes, out of the way of people walking in the shopping malls. It may be semiautomatic; at signal punched out on a keyboard by a clerk, the car may drive itself from the store's "waiting" area to a loading platform. There, it will be loaded with any item too heavy or bulky to be carried by the customer. When shopping is done, the electric cart will be left at the parking-lot gate. The cart, if semiautomatic, will drive itself back to a pickup pool for the next customer to use. Your own car, meanwhile, may also arrive automatically. As mentioned before, the "street" car may be an all-electric or a hybrid electric. As an all-electric, it will be a larger, faster version of the cart, but it will probably look much like one of today's compact gasoline cars. It will have the same roominess and comfort for your drive home. It will travel at faster speeds than the cart. It may be capable of highway travel up to 60 or 70 miles per hour for short distances, a desirable feature if you live in the suburbs.

If it is a hybrid car, it will have a small engine that does two things. First, the engine runs continuously just to keep the batteries charged. Second, on steep grades, or for high-speed travel, the engine assists the batteries in supplying electricity for the drive motors on the wheels. This engine may be either an internal-combustion or an external-combustion type such as a steam engine.

For at least part of the ride home, electric cars of the future may travel in special lanes. In these lanes they may be able to hook into the city power mains. If the car is not a hybrid type, it may have to be able to use such an outside source of power for any long, fast drive to get out of or across the city. It would become a miniature trolley car or one-car "electric train."

On "city" power, the car would probably operate on a different voltage from the one its battery supply delivers. Its motors would probably also operate as AC motors. As discussed previously, with proper automatic switching, a single motor can change its type and accept different voltage or current levels, or even switch between DC and AC. But this arrangement would require expensive design and engineering.

Many experimental models of battery-operated cars of the 1960s and 1970s ran on AC induction motors. A converter device within the car changed DC to AC. Power conversion—from DC to AC or the reverse—is an old story in the electric industry; for cars, the only problem is to make the converter compact as well as efficient. As you saw in the chapter on power plants, a pulsed-DC motor has a great deal in common with an AC motor. Finally, there is no reason why AC from city mains cannot be converted to DC within the car for use by DC motors, of the "pulsed" or of the "continuous" type.

The car you drive home may be your own "second" car, or it may be a leased or rented one. You may be purchasing *transportation,* not cars—as is already being done with the Witkar (page 63). You might or might not use the same car every day. They would all be interchangeable anyway. It would be "your" car while you were using it, but for your next trip you might want to turn it in and get a "fresh" one, cleaned, vacuumed, and equipped with absolutely fresh batteries.

The rental concept might be quite significant in an electric-car era. The rented item might be the car or the batteries. Charging batteries takes time. For long trips, you might pull into a service station to have the entire battery pack changed, rather than charged. In just a few minutes, about the same time a stop for gasoline and oil-checking takes now, attendants would remove the batteries from the car and insert a set of fully charged ones. The cost of the electricity, we can hope, would not be more than the price for gasoline.

A system of renting batteries would overcome one of the major problems of electric cars, that is, the time required to charge batteries. There is really no need to own batteries. Besides, the companies that make the batteries might want to have full control over them. That way the batteries would be more likely to be recycled, rather than making mountains of old

batteries in junkyards. Recycling would be particularly important for batteries containing expensive materials such as silver or
cadmium.

The concept of paying for electricity only can be extended
to renting the cars, and paying for mileage only. Renting
simplifies many things for the car user. For example, the company that actually owns the car is responsible for all maintenance. Renting is not a new idea. Today's rent-a-car companies
operate this way, and each boasts that it tries to give the best
possible maintenance. Long-term leasing of gasoline cars has
been particularly successful in large cities such as New York.
Owning a car presents many problems and renting helps to
overcome them.

Electric cars might change many things. If the idea of
leased or rented electrics takes hold, the entire automobile marketing system might go this way: even the remaining gasoline
cars would be leased. The true owners of the cars might then
take extremely good care of the cars' antipollution devices to
avoid running afoul of the law or provoking the passage of even
stricter laws. Federal antipollution laws seem to be getting
stricter in five-year steps.

Electric cars might also change the pattern of use, and
even of building of roads and streets. Special lanes may be set
aside for them on expressways. They might have other special
lanes into and out of shopping districts. They might be permit-
ted in places where internal-combustion cars will not be permit-
ted at all. More and more cities are building pedestrian shopping malls, served by public transportation or by rather remote
parking lots. Electrics—at least the "free" electric shopping cart
—may have special lanes here, too. Shopping centers, entertainment centers, and streets generally will probably undergo
changes to accommodate different modes of transportation.

Electric cars could significantly change cities in the future,
and the not too distant future, at that. The "electric-car city"

could be a different city from any known now. It will be cleaner, greener, and more quiet, not with the strained stillness of discipline, but with the warm, friendly, quiet of ease, of relaxation. It could be a city that is easy to get around in.

In this city, it will be people who are moving, not so much things. Everything is scaled to people. People move in many ways in this city. Shopping takes place along pedestrian malls, where people stroll from one store to the next. The young and the energetic zing by on bicycles, on their separate paths. Those who are laden or tired ride in taxis or the free shopping-cart cars we have described, perhaps below the level of the foot and bike traffic. Different kinds of traffic do not cross at grade. Some of the pedestrians are even in "tunnel bridges" many stories above the streets, going from one complex of tall buildings to another. The taxis and shopping carts and "rest-your-feet" buses —much like sightseeing buses—are electric.

Fast underground trains (they used to call them subways when they were noisy and dirty) get people to another part of town, or one can take a two-story, open-top excursion bus, also electric. Or the in-town car can be used on special lanes, with a minimum of stop and go. If the city has installed a semiautomatic system for electric cars, perhaps one need only dial the destination into a gadget on the dashboard, and the electric car does the rest. Or a car can easily be rented just by calling for it.

At the end of your shopping or entertainment spree, if you live within the city, your in-town car takes you home and then puts itself in the garage. Tomorrow morning, or whenever you need a car again, this particular car or another just like it will come back if you have reserved it.

For those who live in the suburbs, there is fast intercity transit. Or a "commute" car can be used on special lanes on the expressway. If the car is individually owned, it will sit in a garage overnight to recharge its batteries. If it is leased, arrangements can be made for a fresh car to arrive in the morning, just by pushing the right button on a panel in the house.

People who live far out, in the hinterlands, on a farm or a ranch, are more likely to own their own car, and it may even be an internal-combustion type. Use of internal-combustion cars in the cities may not be allowed. Most traffic in the towns will be smog-free, noise-free, and probably electric. The *old-fashioned*, long-distance, high-speed gasoline car might travel on special lanes, through or around a city. The internal-combustion driver would switch over to an electric runabout in the city. As is the case today, the "classic" car is big, for long-distance comfort. But even today it is too much to handle in a city.

The accent in this "new" city will be on keeping people and goods moving as people want to move, not on handling problems that come with having too many over-big, over-powered, noisy, fume-emitting cars in one small space. A theater-goer, for example, as he gets out of his electric car in front of the theater, would push a button on the car's dashboard labeled "Park." The car then hooks into the city's control system and goes and parks itself until it is needed.

This may seem like a visionary's vision indeed. But the electric car brings the possibilities down to earth, makes some visionary ideas practical.

It is true that the electric-car-centered city of the future described here would require massive doses of money, effort, and technological expertise—in effect, a whole new technology. It may sound impossible, but a whole new technology was developed to take advantage of petroleum. Fifty years ago, the present system of interstate highways and freeways seemed like a visionary's dream, indeed. But enough people wanted, or at least thought they wanted, automobiles to make millions of automobiles and the highways on which to run them a reality. So if enough people want pollution free transportation in the form of electric cars enough to pay for it, they will have it. It is only a matter of time.

Index

E. John De Waard, the author of *The Color of Life*, has been a teacher of elementary, high school, and college students for many years. He has also been a writer and an editor of children's books and newspapers. Born in Michigan, Mr. De Waard received an A.B. degree in science at Adrian College, and a Master's degree in biology from Michigan State University. At present he works for a publishing house in California and lives there with his wife and two sons.

Aaron E. Klein, author of *Threads of Life* and *The Hidden Contributors*, taught biology in secondary schools and colleges for over ten years. Born in Atlanta, Georgia, he was educated in Georgia and Connecticut, the Universities of Pennsylvania and Bridgeport, and Yale and Wesleyan Universities. He participated in the Visiting Scientist Program of the Museum of Art, Science, and Industry in Bridgeport, Connecticut. At present he is managing editor of a classroom science newspaper. Mr. Klein lives in Connecticut with his wife and two sons.